59 Reasons to Write

Mini-Lessons, Prompts, and Inspiration for Teachers

kate messner

STENHOUSE PUBLISHERS
PORTLAND, MAINE

Stenhouse Publishers
www.stenhouse.com

Library of Congress Cataloging-in-Publication Data

Messner, Kate.
59 reasons to write : mini-lessons, prompts, and inspiration for teachers / Kate Messner.
pages cm
Includes bibliographical references and index.
ISBN 978-1-62531-003-3 (pbk. : alk. paper) -- ISBN 978-1-62531-038-5 (ebook) 1. English language--Composition and exercises--Study and teaching. 2. Creative writing. 3. English language--Rhetoric. I. Title. II. Title: Fifty-nine reasons to write.
LB1576.M4568 2014
808'.042071--dc23
2014024897

Cover design, interior design by Blue Design, Portland, Maine (www.bluedes.com)

Manufactured in the United States of America

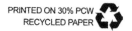

PRINTED ON 30% PCW
RECYCLED PAPER

21 20 19 18 17 16 15   9 8 7 6 5 4 3 2 1

For Jennifer Vincent, Gae Polisner, Jo Knowles, and all the members of our Teachers Write community: it is such a gift to know you, write with you, and learn with you.

CONTENTS

Acknowledgments

At the end of the day, this is a book meant to celebrate writing communities, and I am so very thankful for mine. This project wouldn't exist without the generosity of all of our Teachers Write guest authors and Q-and-A Wednesday guests whose words are featured throughout the book. Your willingness to share your time and talent is very much appreciated. Special thanks go to Gae Polisner, Jennifer Vincent, and Jo Knowles, who have led our online writing camp with me from the start.

My trade book publishers, Bloomsbury, Chronicle, and Scholastic, have been incredibly supportive of my work in mentoring teacher-writers through our online camp and resources for this book. Thanks to my editors, Anamika Bhatnagar, Mary Kate Castellani, Melissa Manlove, and Cassandra Pelham, and my agent, Jennifer Laughran, for all that you've shared for this project and for all that you've taught me about writing and revising.

I'm grateful to Holly Holland at Stenhouse for encouraging me to write this book and then waiting until I had the time to do it right, and to Chris Downey, Chandra Lowe, and the rest of the terrific Stenhouse team. I also want to thank my team at home—Tom, Jake, and Ella—for making space for me to do the work that I love and for being patient when I'm staring off into the distance thinking about Chapter 4 instead of answering a question someone asked me five minutes earlier.

For this book, I owe the biggest debt of gratitude to the teachers and librarians who asked for the Teachers Write summer camp in the first place. You showed up in droves to participate and nurtured this online community as if every member were one of your beloved students or colleagues, even though we were spread all over the world. You shared your writing, your fears, your joys, and your hearts. Without you, this book wouldn't exist. Thank you for that—and more. I learned so very much from all of you and am thankful to call you colleagues and friends.

Contributors

Sarah Albee
Gigi Amateau
Jeannine Atkins
Pam Bachorz
Phil Bildner
Jennifer Brown
Loree Griffin Burns
Nancy Castaldo
Shutta Crum
Karen Day
Erin Dealey
Kristy Dempsey
Jaclyn Dolamore
Katy Duffield
Jody Feldman
Miriam Forster
D. Dina Friedman
Donna Gephart
Amy Guglielmo
Danette Haworth
Sara Lewis Holmes
Lynda Mullaly Hunt
Mike Jung
Lynne Kelly
Jo Knowles
Joanne Levy
Sarah Darer Littman
Dayna Lorentz
Natalie Dias Lorenzi
David Lubar
Melissa Manlove
Jenny Meyerhoff
Donalyn Miller
Megan Miranda
Anne Marie Pace
A. J. Paquette
Rosanne Parry
Gae Polisner
Jean Reidy
Caroline Starr Rose
Barb Rosenstock
Elizabeth Rusch
Lisa Schroeder
Laurel Snyder
Margo Sorenson
Linda Urban
Jennifer Vincent
Pamela Voelkel
Sally Wilkins
Laura Wynkoop
Brian Wyzlic
Diane Zahler

CHAPTER 1

Introduction

Lake Champlain froze this week, and the ice outside my writing room window is perfectly midnight-blue clear. It's smooth and finally thick enough for skating. It's talking, too. Otherworldly gurgles and booms echo off the rocks, so loud I can hear them even at my desk. What I hear most is "Come outside. Come skate."

The glorious new lake ice pulls at me today, but if it weren't the ice, it would be something else—probably something far less enchanting, like grocery shopping or emails to answer or kitchen counters to clean. I can think of a thousand reasons not to write. You probably can, too. There are papers to grade, evaluations to fill out, kids to drive to soccer practice, cookies to bake, clothes to wash, and if all that gets done, two episodes of *Downton Abbey* are waiting on the DVR. So how could there be time to write?

I meet lots of teachers, librarians, and readers when I travel for conferences and school visits. Many of you confide that you have stories you need to tell, poems you hope to write, and ideas you want to share. And then, many of you say, "I really want to write, but . . ."

I really want to write, but I can't find the time.

I really want to write, but I don't know how to get started.

I really want to write, but teaching leaves me exhausted at the end of the day.

I really want to write, but I'm afraid it won't be good enough.

I really want to write, but . . .

Here is a secret about writing. If you really want to write, you can write. And now is the best time to begin.

If you're a teacher or librarian who feels guilty about time spent away from your professional obligations, it may help to look at writing as an essential part of your work in being a teacher of writing. Because it is.

Before I became a full-time writer, I taught middle school English for fifteen years—a career I chose because I had loved reading books and writing stories as a kid. As an adult, I loved teaching writing just as much. For every new piece I assigned my students, I'd create a model for them, a sample essay or story or poem to help them understand the expectations for the assignment.

But a few years into my teaching career, something changed. It started when I was looking for a work of historical fiction about a particular Revolutionary War battle on Lake Champlain and couldn't find one that would be accessible to my students. I asked around at the library and local museums but came up empty. "Maybe you should write it yourself," someone suggested, half joking. But that idea took hold, and I began scribbling ideas. Those ideas turned into research. I read piles of books and journals and letters, interviewed experts, and took part in a battle reenactment with a local maritime museum. After seven years of research, writing, revision, rejections, and more revision, a small regional publisher picked up my historical novel, and I finally had the story I'd wished for, to share with my students.

I also had a new outlook on teaching, because when I got serious about my own writing, everything changed. Suddenly, I wasn't the all-knowing expert any more. I was struggling sometimes, agonizing over characters whose motivations didn't ring true, details from history that completely derailed my plot, chapter endings that felt forced. I made the choice to bring all of those challenges into my classroom, to share my struggles with my students. It was huge, and I learned something important.

Writing *for* my students provided me with appropriate mentor texts to share.

Writing *with* my students made me a mentor and a far better teacher. Because I was in the middle of the messy process, just as they were, I understood the feeling of *wanting* to finish but being stuck. I could relate to their fear and their failures—and that made all of our successes so much more to celebrate.

That's why I took notice of a particular conversation on Twitter in the spring of 2012. Jennifer Vincent, a teacher I'd met at a conference, said that she really wanted to spend time on her own writing over the coming summer, and that she wished there were some kind of a support group. A few other educators chimed in, and I responded with an off-the-cuff offer to host an online summer writing camp for teachers and librarians. It would be fun, free, and super-casual—just a place where teachers and librarians who wanted to work on their writing could come together, get some inspiration and strategies from published authors, and share their progress.

The response was positive—"We'd love that!"—and the result was Teachers Write, a free, virtual summer writing camp for educators and librarians. I enlisted the help of a wonderful group of children's authors and set up a weekly schedule for our online workshop. Author Jo Knowles shared a warm-up exercise to start us off each week. Mini-Lesson Mondays featured workshops on craft that covered everything from brainstorming and outlining to researching nonfiction. Tuesdays and Thursdays were Quick-Write days, with writing prompts that could be used to generate new ideas or extend thinking for a work in progress. On Q-and-A Wednesdays, teachers and librarians could ask questions of me and guest authors who popped in to visit. And Fridays were . . . well . . . Fridays. We called it Writing Happy Hour, and used the last day of the week to celebrate the work we'd done together, passing around virtual lemonade, offering book giveaways, and sharing accomplishments and struggles from the week.

Young adult author Gae Polisner also hosted Friday Feedback on her blog, giving anyone the chance to share a few paragraphs they'd written and to give and receive feedback. We took weekends off, but Jennifer Vincent invited participants to stop by her blog on Sundays to talk about their writing and the impact that writing might have on their teaching.

When I first posted the news about Teachers Write on my blog, I expected maybe a dozen teachers and librarians to join. It would be fun, low-key, and cozy. But soon after I shared that invitation, it became clear that the program would be bigger than I'd thought. Sixty people signed up in the first hour, and within a few days, that number swelled to six hundred. The week after our virtual writing camp began, we were more than a thousand writers strong. That's when I stopped keeping count and simply marveled at the enthusiasm, passion, talent, and courage showing up in the comments of my blog every day.

Our "cozy little online writing camp" was no longer small, but it was doing what I'd hoped it would do: encouraging and supporting teachers and librarians who wanted to be better writers. Our first summer was nothing short of inspirational. It renewed my belief that teachers are the most passionate lifelong learners of all and that even in the face of dwindling professional development funds, they'll seek out and create their own opportunities for growth.

More Reasons to Keep Writing

The purpose of this book is to extend that summer writing camp magic by sharing what we did, what we learned, and what we created, and to provide a framework for a writing program that can be run in any school district or community. The lessons and prompts in this book can be done in any order that works best for you. They can be used to run a writing group of any size, run by anyone who wants to support teachers and librarians as writers and as mentors for the young writers they serve. Really, this book isn't just for teachers and librarians. It's for anyone who's always wanted to write, but . . .

So here are fifty-nine reasons to write: lessons and writing prompts ranging from a character's flaws to the memory of a kitchen from your past. Write, because you have things to say—arguments to make, stories to tell, poems to share—and no one else in the world has your unique voice with which to say them. And do it for the young writers you hope to inspire. In making time for your own writing, you'll be crossing a barrier, joining them as real, vulnerable members of a community of writers.

There will always be a world tugging us away from our notebooks or laptops. There will always be hesitation about getting started, worries about whether it's good enough, and challenges when it comes to finding a quiet spot to put words on paper. But if you really want to write, you can write. And you should start today.

How to Use This Book

The mini-lessons, essays, and prompts in this book are organized in chapters by topic. Although you might organize your writing workshop that way, too, kicking off with a week of Getting Started lessons and then moving into organization, setting, character, and so on, you might also find that you'd rather have more variety each week, such as working a bit with setting on Monday and Tuesday, then exploring poetry on Wednesday, and focusing on nonfiction for the rest of the week. Whether you're writing alone, with a small group of friends or colleagues, or with your whole school district, this reproducible chart will allow you to schedule ten weeks of writing workshop based on your interests and needs. See Figure 1.1 for a sample schedule.

FIGURE 1.1

Sample writing workshop schedule

WEEK/DAY	DATE	LESSON / ASSIGNMENT	PAGE #
Week 1-Monday			
Week 1-Tuesday			
Week 1-Wednesday			
Week 1-Thursday			
Week 1-Friday			
Week 2-Monday			
Week 2-Tuesday			
Week 2-Wednesday			
Week 2-Thursday			
Week 2-Friday			
Week 3-Monday			
Week 3-Tuesday			
Week 3-Wednesday			
Week 3-Thursday			
Week 3-Friday			
Week 4-Monday			
Week 4-Tuesday			
Week 4-Wednesday			
Week 4-Thursday			
Week 4-Friday			
Week 5-Monday			
Week 5-Tuesday			
Week 5-Wednesday			

Week 5-Thursday			
Week 5-Friday			
Week 6-Monday			
Week 6-Tuesday			
Week 6-Wednesday			
Week 6-Thursday			
Week 6-Friday			
Week 7-Monday			
Week 7-Tuesday			
Week 7-Wednesday			
Week 7-Thursday			
Week 7-Friday			
Week 8-Monday			
Week 8-Tuesday			
Week 8-Wednesday			
Week 8-Thursday			
Week 8-Friday			
Week 9-Monday			
Week 9-Tuesday			
Week 9-Wednesday			
Week 9-Thursday			
Week 9-Friday			
Week 10-Monday			
Week 10-Tuesday			
Week 10-Wednesday			
Week 10-Thursday			
Week 10-Friday			

Kate Messner is the award-winning author of more than two dozen current and forthcoming books for young readers, including picture books, nonfiction, chapter books, and novels. A former middle school English teacher, Kate earned National Board Certification in Early Adolescent English Language Arts in 2006. She honed her writing craft alongside her students and still loves visiting schools to conduct writing workshops with kids and teachers alike. Kate's first book for teachers and writers, *Real Revision: Authors' Strategies to Share with Student Writers* (Stenhouse 2011), focuses on making the revision process accessible and fun. Kate is a frequent keynote speaker at events for educators, librarians, and writers, and was a featured speaker at the 2012 TED conference. Her TED talk was later animated as a TED-Ed video on world building in fiction and has garnered close to a million views online as of this writing.

Kate lives on Lake Champlain with her family, and when she's not writing or reading, she loves spending time outside. Follow her on Twitter @KateMessner, and learn more at her website: www.katemessner.com.

KATE'S BOOKS FOR YOUNG READERS

Picture Books

How to Read a Story (Chronicle 2015)

Up in the Garden and Down in the Dirt (Chronicle 2015)

Tree of Wonder: The Many Marvelous Lives of a Rainforest Tree (Chronicle 2015)

Sea Monster and the Bossy Fish (Chronicle 2013)

Over and Under the Snow (Chronicle 2011)

Sea Monster's First Day (Chronicle 2011)

Chapter Books

Ranger in Time: Rescue on the Oregon Trail (Scholastic 2015)

Ranger in Time: Danger in Ancient Rome (Scholastic 2015)

Marty McGuire Has Too Many Pets! (Scholastic 2014)

Marty McGuire Digs Worms (Scholastic 2012)

Marty McGuire (Scholastic 2011)

Novels

All the Answers (Bloomsbury 2015)

Manhunt (Scholastic 2014)

Hide and Seek **(Scholastic 2013)**

Wake Up Missing **(Bloomsbury 2013)**

Capture the Flag **(Scholastic 2012)**

Eye of the Storm **(Bloomsbury 2012)**

Sugar and Ice **(Bloomsbury 2010)**

The Brilliant Fall of Gianna Z. **(Bloomsbury 2009)**

The Best of Q-and-A Wednesday: Beginnings

Q-and-A Wednesday was a tradition in our summertime Teachers Write workshops. We had specific topics for mini-lessons and prompts on most days of the week, but every Wednesday, when published authors visited for Q and A, the floor was open for questions about almost anything that has to do with writing. That free-for-all led to some wonderful conversations, and I've included some of my favorite exchanges in this book, as they relate to the chapter themes.

You'll find these comments throughout the book; please feel free to share them with your writing groups and with your student writers. Some of the conversations include writing tips, strategies, and problem-solving ideas. Others share stories and challenges, and these are no less helpful to emerging writers. Sometimes, simply hearing that a professional has the same struggles is enough to keep a writer coming back to that imperfect page.

Q+A - THE BEST OF Q-AND-A WEDNESDAY: WRITING ROUTINES

What does a writer really do, anyway? What does a typical day look like? We asked our guest authors all about their writing lives, wondering what kinds of writing settings and habits are most likely to call the muse.

QUESTION: What environment do you write in? Music on? Shut in a closet? Lots of snacks handy? I'd love to share with my students to help them as writers.

ANSWERS:

Sometimes I need it to be completely quiet. Other times, the music is going (like right now—Jay Z), the television is on, and I have six or seven tabs open in my browser. I like to write in different places. I write in my apartment, on the subway (great for people-watching), and outside on the roof deck.

Finally, when I'm doing late-stage revisions, I need to read my work out loud. I'll even play dress-up when I do that!

~Phil Bildner, author of *The Soccer Fence*

Like Phil, I often write in different places. These days I'm usually outside near my pool with my big dog. I don't eat snacks while I'm writing, but I love to reward myself with a piece of chocolate when I'm finished. Rewards can be fun. I like to reward myself every step of the way–including when I finish a chapter or send off a proposal. The reward isn't always chocolate–sometimes it might be a hike in a nearby nature preserve or tea with a friend. I always believe that it's important to set goals and acknowledge those accomplished. Plus it adds fun to a solitary business!

~Nancy Castaldo, author of *Sniffer Dogs: How Dogs (and Their Noses) Save the World*

I tend to keep one CD in the player for months, if not years. Currently, I'm listening to Tab Benoit's Fever for the Bayou. *I'll also listen to Bach, Vivaldi, or Doc Watson. Sometimes, I can only listen to instrumental music. (I think that the familiarity of a CD that I play repeatedly, like Tab Benoit's, helps keep the words from being a distraction.) I am constantly interrupted by cats. I am occasionally interrupted by the delivery of an unexpected but much appreciated snack.*

However, I think it is important to also let your students know that each writer's process, as far as things that are removed from the actual mechanics and art of writing and revising, is an individual preference that should not be seen as a means to an end. Questions about personal habits as part of the process always make me think of the great Borges story "Pierre Menard, Author of the Quixote," about a man who tried to re-create the writing of that book.

~David Lubar, author of *Hidden Talents* and the Weenies short story collections

QUESTION: Can you tell us about your personal, daily writing schedule?

ANSWERS:

For about eight years, I wrote while also working full-time for an educational publisher. Back then, I scheduled my writing time religiously. I committed to at least ten hours per week. I kept a stack of blank grids in my study, and each Friday I planned the following week. I wrote down exercise time (at least three times a week) and also writing time. Then I posted it on my study door so my family could see it, too. The schedule varied from week to week. Sometimes I'd wake up at five or six to write until my son was up. Other times I'd "binge" with big blocks of time on the weekend. It all depended on what else was going on in my week.

Then, about a year ago, my employer very wonderfully agreed to let me transition to a part-

time schedule. Now I write every weekday morning for at least three hours, and then I work every weekday afternoon for about four and a half hours. I can't tell you how much I love this schedule, and how lucky I feel. My writing has transformed. Before, I was so tired, and I felt so rushed. Now I have these lovely long and predictable blocks when I can create.

~Pam Bachorz, author of *Candor* and *Drought*

It seems like it's never the same two days in a row. I started writing before my older son was born, so for eight years of writing, I had to work around babies/toddlers/preschoolers. I usually stayed up super-late or got up super-early and definitely wrote through naptimes and during the short hours they were at preschool.

But three years ago, two things happened. I finally got published, and my youngest went off to kindergarten, and I found myself with way *too much time on my hands. My schedule was no longer dictated to me, and I was very unproductive that first year. Fortunately, I've had some time to work it out.*

I am still a stay-at-home mom, first and foremost, so I never even try to write during a time that my kids need my attention (for example, I'm not writing much this summer; only in little spurts and fits when they're off at a camp or sleeping over at a friend's house, etc.). I find this to be the easiest way to keep from feeling pulled in too many directions.

I also lose at least one writing day per month (and sometimes–usually in October and May–several days per month) to school and library visits. I just accept that these things are an important part of the job, and I don't try to write on those days, either.

But on a day where I actually have all day to write, it kind of goes like this: I start by answering emails and filling out interviews for blogs and so forth. I update my Facebook and Twitter. Then I take a break for a workout. This is important, because it helps me clear my mind. I come back, grab some lunch, and get writing. I write for about four hours, but find that after much more than four hours, I start to get "stale." I need some pondering time in between scenes, and if I'm cranking away for longer than four hours, I just don't get that important pondering time. I try to have it all done and put away before the kids get out of school, and then I check emails and Facebook and Twitter and all that stuff again before bedtime.

~Jennifer Brown, author of *Hate List*

I work full-time, and because that takes up a good portion of my weekdays, I do most of my writing on weekends. I need fairly large uninterrupted chunks of time to draft, so most of that is done on weekends, but I am okay editing in the evenings after work.

~Joanne Levy, author of *Small Medium at Large*

Me? I get up, eat bon bons for breakfast, write a few bon mots, and then have my hunky cabana boy feed me grapes while I get a full-body massage.

And then I wake up to my real life. I've learned to write anytime, anywhere, anyplace. This is probably how I've developed tendonitis and carpal tunnel syndrome in my wrists. I've written parts of my novels in doctor's office waiting rooms. This morning I was writing (and answering some of these questions) while my daughter was having physiotherapy. My author bio includes the title "unpaid chauffeur," and as a single parent, that role has dominated my life for a very long time. I'm not sure who is more excited about my daughter training to get her license in the next few months–her or me!

I use the Freedom app to "turn off the Internet" for periods of time–sometimes fifteen minutes, sometimes thirty, sometimes an hour, depending on the day. I write like a fiend during the offline time, then allow myself a quick online break, then turn the Internet off again.

Although I don't have a "day job," I do political writing as well as novels. Sometimes it's hard to switch gears when I've got a column due.

I try to go to one retreat a year where I can be a hard-core writer. I get more done at that retreat in three days than in three weeks at home.

~Sarah Darer Littman, author of *Want to Go Private?* and *Backlash*

When I was teaching full-time, my writing schedule involved getting the kids to bed, writing from 9:00 to 11:00 p.m. or until I couldn't keep my eyes open any more, and then going to bed. Rinse and repeat. I did this on weekdays, and weekends were mixed: sometimes I'd take them off to relax and have family time, or if I really needed to get work done, I'd head out to a coffee shop for a few hours during the day.

Now that I'm no longer teaching, I write from about 10:30 to 2:30 every day, sometimes again at night. That's during the school year. During the summer, I'm incredibly sporadic and will go a few days without writing much but then put in a twelve-hour day if I'm on deadline.

~Kate Messner, author of *All the Answers, How to Read a Story,* and the Ranger in Time series

I think it's a good idea to schedule your "intense writing time" for the time of day that you, personally, are most productive. I am a morning person, so I get up at 4:30–5:00 or so, allow myself ten–fifteen minutes to check email and Facebook, walk the dog, accept the cup of coffee that my husband has lovingly brewed for me, and get to work. During the school year, I work until seven, when the kids get up, and then get back to work after the morning craziness for another three or four hours. If I've met my writing quota for the day (which varies, depending on the project and my adrenaline level/freak-out mode about a deadline), I allow myself to do less structured stuff, like writing a blog post, answering emails, exercising, and life maintenance. If I'm lucky, I can squeeze in another chunk of writing time later in the day, but that's a bonus.

~Sarah Albee, author of *Poop Happened: A History of the World from the Bottom Up* and *Bugged: How Insects Changed History*

I don't have a real routine, but I try to write every day, even if I think what I'm writing isn't working. The next day, I go back and polish (or delete). If I'm really stuck, I keep on anyway but file the problem mentally until I'm in the car on a long drive or on a long walk. Movement seems to free my brain to work out problems. I used to drive my son to school forty-five minutes away, and that daily one and a half hours in the car was great for fixing my writing. If I can work it out mentally, then it flows onto paper (or computer). What's important—for me, anyway—is getting the words down. They can always be changed or improved (or deleted).

~Diane Zahler, author of *Sleeping Beauty's Daughters* and *The Black Death*

If I get really stuck and I hate what I'm doing, I try to still write something *on it every day. If it's really bad, I might make a pretty modest goal, like three hundred words. Then when I've written three hundred words, I allow myself to work on something more fun or even just go do something else entirely. Sometimes you do have to step away and put a project on the back burner to work itself out in the subconscious, but it's also a fine line between putting something on the back burner and procrastinating forever or giving up. So if the project I'm stuck on is my number one project, I try not to let it go entirely. I've found that forcing myself to write even a little bit every day also forces me to keep thinking about how to solve the problem until I get a lightbulb moment.*

I also find that certain activities trigger lightbulb moments more often, like taking a shower or reading a really good novel in a similar genre or a book that has some research-related pertinence to whatever I'm writing.

~Jaclyn Dolamore, author of *Magic Under Glass* and *Dark Metropolis*

During the school year (when all is quiet in the house), I have a routine that I stick to. It begins with getting the kids ready, and the rest of the schedule falls like dominoes. I have a set time that I must start writing. Sometimes, I am really dragging, working hard but gaining very little distance; other days, the words flow, and I hit word counts that shock me (not usually the case, though!). I find that having a routine keeps my mind primed, same as a regular exercise routine keeps the body primed.

Now, summer is different altogether! Activities, visitors (I live in Florida, an hour from Disney and Cocoa Beach), and vacations throw my writing schedule way off. I try not to feel bad about that. My kids are only young once, but I'll always be a writer.

~Danette Haworth, author of *A Whole Lot of Lucky* and *Violet Raines Almost Got Struck by Lightning*

Two Teachers Writing

When teachers come together as part of a writing community, magical things happen, not just for the teacher-writers but also for the student writers with whom they work. Two of the most active participants in our summer Teachers Write camp started the process as strangers but ended up forming an across-the-miles online critique and support group. Jennifer Vincent and Brian Wyzlic reflect on how writing together and writing regularly have transformed their teaching as well.

JEN

In two summers of Teachers Write, I grew remarkably as a writer. The community and camaraderie helped me be more motivated, focused, and confident in my own writing, and to understand more about writing in general. Kate, Gae, Jo, and the many other authors and bookish professionals who gave their time, energy, and ideas to Teachers Write are amazing. Thanks to their insights, I wrote more, tried new things in my writing, and asked questions I never thought to ask before. Not only did I benefit from the whole community, but I was lucky enough to connect with Brian as a mini-critique-writing-support-group partner (or Maquizga, as we call it now). I am more conscious of what I need to be a productive writer and what students might need in terms of support, advice, and feedback. It's amazing to look back on two summers of Teachers Write and realize the extent of the impact it has had on us.

BRIAN

My whole approach to how I write and how I teach writing has changed because of Teachers Write. Before, I just sort of did what I thought needed to be done based on what previous teachers in my position had done. I had minimal training in teaching writing. After going through Teachers Write, I found out what it means to write—what it means to be a writer. This fundamentally changed how I approached my writing students for the better.

JEN

When I think about writing throughout my entire life, I realize I had an awesome experience in school. I had a fifth-grade teacher who journaled back and forth with students regularly. From sixth grade through high school, I had teachers who led reading and writing workshop. The whole idea that writing is a process has always made sense to me because of these great teachers and my experience with the workshop model. After high school, I didn't do much narrative writing. In college, I wrote mostly research papers, and then I started blogging after I had been teaching for a few years. My blog has been devoted to personal narrative, reflection pieces, and nonfiction around literacy and teaching.

In 2011, I saw many Twitter friends talking about NaNoWriMo, which stands for National Novel Writing Month. Every November, people take on the challenge to write a novel, or at least a fifty-thousand-word draft, that month. I decided I would go for it. I hadn't written fiction since high school, but I was excited to at least try. I had read Ralph Fletcher's work on writer's notebooks and had started them with my students, but this felt like an opportunity to really live the life of a writer in order to model and support students in writing. That's when I started to get serious about writing a novel and getting back into fiction writing. I didn't "win" NaNoWriMo, but the desire to finish the first draft of my novel and to share it with students was what brought me to Teachers Write.

BRIAN

I came to writing from a different angle. I didn't think much of writing until I was in high school, where I found a lot of solace in writing poetry and short stories. I thought I was good, until I got to college and took a creative writing class. Turns out I had *much* to learn! But my writing sort of took a backseat to everything else in my life, and at some point, it just fell out the back of the car.

Reading was what reawakened the stories in me, and I knew I would have to write. What I didn't have were the tools to work on the craft and develop myself as a writer, and as a writing teacher for my students.

JEN

Yes! I completely agree that reading so many books helped me know stories and see how I can extend my love of reading into writing. I wholeheartedly believe in mentor texts, and reading voraciously gave me a great foundation for writing. This is another belief about supporting student writers. Encouraging students to read more and to interact with text as readers helps to build their foundation and understanding of how words fit together and how stories unfold. Matching this exposure to text and talking about text with looking closely at mentor texts and examining an author's craft is best practice in supporting students as much as it has helped me as a writer.

BRIAN

It seems like there were countless ways to develop as a reader, though not many places exist to develop as a writer, especially from a teacher's perspective. That's why I'm so glad Teachers Write came to be.

JEN

Since being part of Teachers Write, I've discovered numerous resources for writing, including the Society of Children's Book Writers and Illustrators and the National Writing Project. I read books by Ralph Fletcher and Jeff Anderson about writing and devoured Kate's book *Real Revision* when it was published, but I also learned about other books on writing that weren't specific to teachers. Books such as *On Writing* by Stephen King, *Bird by Bird* by Anne Lamott, and *Save the Cat* by Blake Snyder have all added to what I know and understand about writing and what I can bring to students in terms of writing.

At the end of every week, I reflected on my writing and made plans for the week to come. Teachers Write participants were invited to my blog to do this weekly check-in with me. The Teachers Write friends who visited my blog on Sundays and shared their experiences helped me celebrate my ups and downs throughout the writing process and think deeply about myself as a writer. I love this weekly reflection and believe that it helped me learn how to trust my instincts about writing and how to push myself as a writer.

The weekly check-in helped me pay attention to myself as a writer. The Teachers Write Sunday Check-In helped me know and understand myself as a writer but also gave me this clear understanding of how to confer with students and to facilitate their thinking about themselves as writers. By doing the weekly check-in, I also recognized what was working for me, and insights into writing that I might model to support student writers.

BRIAN

The community was a huge part of Teachers Write for me; it may have been the biggest asset that a lot of other "writing tips" websites don't have. Friday Feedback was something that really brought me together with a lot of other people, both published authors and unpublished writers. Being able to not only see what other people were writing but share my own in a nurturing environment was something I'd never really experienced before, aside from a small workshop class I had in college. The rule of keeping positive and giving only feedback people asked for was great for me as an emerging writer, and it became an incredible policy to bring to the classroom.

JEN

I love Friday Feedback for exactly this reason. I was determined to complete the first draft of my novel, but along the way, being able to share my writing on Gae's blog encouraged me to keep going. I totally get that a first draft isn't going to be perfect and that it's all about getting something down on the page, but I was new at writing. I thrived on cheerleading. There were many times when Gae and others would say, "Keep going!" and I believed I could. There were other times when I received specific feedback that I could apply to my writing. For example, sometimes Gae would do a quick edit and show how I could really make my writing more concise. I'm a super-verbose person, and it's easy for me to repeat one word twelve times in a sentence or to describe something that is obvious to the reader.

Many Teachers Write participants talked about how scared they were to share their writing. It's not easy to share our writing because it is so connected to who we are. Because I've participated in writing workshop before and I blog, it didn't scare me to share my writing. I was more excited to get feedback than anything else. Hearing someone else's feedback really helps me know how to adjust my writing to be better for my reader, and this is how I grow as a writer.

BRIAN

All of the things you mentioned here—the cheerleading, the specific feedback, the safe place to share, and the ability to grow to accept criticism—are a huge part of Teachers Write but also very important to our students. Teachers Write gave me a chance to experience what my students experience in their writing class every day.

Having felt the support firsthand from experienced authors, I know how important it is that I support my students in what they're writing, even if both they and I know it's not that good yet. I picture a net of support, built with positive feedback and cheerleading. That net grows stronger with every fiber of positive response I give to my students. That net is what they have to fall back on when they receive criticism about their work. Teachers Write made me ask myself, As a teacher, am I giving my students enough support that they have the confidence to accept criticism from their classmates or me? At times, I was. At other times, I was not. And, not surprisingly, the students who were better because of my feedback were those I was nurturing more along the way. It seems obvious, but that's something I didn't really realize before Teachers Write.

The type of feedback I gave changed through Teachers Write, too. I took a creative writing class in high school, and another one in college. That was the extent of my training in teaching creative writing, and it was more than seven years later by the time I taught my own English course. I was a bit rusty, not just on how to give feedback, but on the type of feedback to give. The feedback I got from Gae and other authors on Friday Feedback helped me see what experienced authors and editors do when they offer feedback and criticism. Gae, in particular, showed herself to be masterful with offering feedback about narration, voice, and word choice. I can recall on a few different occasions her telling me that she wasn't sure my character of a somewhat sarcastic teenage boy would actually use flowery language to describe a sunrise. Such feedback I could immediately bring back to my students as I helped them with their works.

JEN

When it comes to giving feedback to students and cheering them along, I notice that students relate to me differently after I tell them that I write, too. This year, students said that they feel more comfortable talking about their writing and coming to ask for help. That is such a huge compliment.

Teachers Write helped me rediscover my love for free writing. When I was in high school, we did all sorts of warm-up exercises for writing. Free writing was always my favorite because it helped me get my ideas out and on the paper. The nature of free writing is to not feel confined by grammar or spelling, complete sentences, or well-crafted thoughts. It's about just getting ideas down, getting them down fast, and letting them loose. By the end of the process, I always feel better. First of all, I feel like I've accomplished something, but I also feel like I have something to work with. I've heard people complain about writer's block, but I have found that by trusting in free writing, I've been able to keep going with my writing one way or another.

Setting up a three- to four-minute free writing time at the beginning of every writing session seems to help students feel more confident. I modeled how to free write at the beginning of the school year, using a document camera. Students watched me as I frantically wrote down ideas, made spelling errors, jumped from one idea to another, and let my ideas go. We had fun laughing about the topic, and they wanted to add their own ideas. They were so excited to write. Seeing me write sloppily, knowing that it was okay to write haphazardly, was a relief. I made it clear to them that free writing is all about the ideas, but I did tell them we would come back to work on everything else later.

Teachers Write has given me the support I need to think through my writing habits, to learn from others, to make myself better along the way, and to share these insights with my students.

BRIAN

I'm so glad Jen and I connected through Teachers Write and as Maquizgas! That has helped me in my writing, just having someone there to say to me, "Did you write today?" This attitude, this culture of having someone to help you with your writing and push you through the dry spells, is something I brought to my classroom as well.

The creative writing class I taught was small, but there were definitely pairs or even groups of three students that formed naturally. I capitalized on this, thinking of the writing-partner relationship Jen and I have, and I had students share with each other what they were writing. We also talked about how to give feedback. These students formed their own community of writers, where they were able to find a safe place to explore their writing and find the push they needed to keep going.

Because we had this organic community in our class, we were able to do more things collaboratively. We talked about plotting out the story, and character development. We had students take turns writing from different characters' perspectives. Through sharing, we saw a story take shape. What started as a story about a high schooler whose parents were divorced turned into a trans-Atlantic trip where long-lost relatives found each other, and we saw our character grow up before our eyes. We never finished the story, largely because of time constraints of the class, but we really grew as a community and as writers through this experience.

JEN

It all comes back to community! Teachers Write helped bring us together as writing partners who can support each other and spur each other on, but it also brings us other teachers who are sharing similar experiences with writing, and amazing authors and other book-world people who can share their insight and expertise. Being surrounded by this wonderful community helps me feel like a writer . . . helps me know I am a writer. This is the best message I can send to students. See me? I am a writer. I'm just a regular person who is also a writer. It helps them see that even if they think they are just regular kids, they are writers, too.

Jen Vincent worked with students who are deaf and hard of hearing for ten years and earned National Board Certification in Early and Middle Childhood Literacy. She works as the coordinator of instructional technology for School District U-46 in Elgin, Illinois. Jen inspires teachers to make learning authentic for students, take risks, and reflect on practice as they integrate technology into instruction. Above all, she models the growth mind-set and builds trusting relationships with teachers to continuously move them toward best practices. She is an active, founding member of Teachers Write, tweets at @mentortexts, and blogs at www.teachmentortexts.com.

Brian Wyzlic teaches grades six through twelve math and English in Hale, Michigan. He strives to bring out the best in his students, modeling for them how to become better writers, readers, mathematicians, and people, both in and out of the classroom. Brian has found that building relationships is the core of his work with students. He is active in the English education community and can be found tweeting at @brianwyzlic.

Jo's Monday Morning Warm-Ups

When you're diving into a new pursuit, it's sometimes best to start with a small assignment, so that's how we'll begin each chapter of this book. Sometimes the morning warm-ups relate directly to the theme of the chapter, and sometimes they don't. It's good to mix things up. That's how we eased into each week of the Teachers Write virtual summer writing camp, too, thanks to guest author Jo Knowles. Every Monday, she got us started writing with a gentle prompt. Here, Jo shares how a tradition that started years ago on her blog has led to the formation of a true writing community.

JO

I began posting Monday Morning Warm-Ups on my blog in 2004. Two of my writing friends had commented, wishing they had writing exercises to do. Because I already shared these warm-ups from time to time, I decided to make them a regular feature. I chose Mondays because it was the day many of us were trying to get back into the writing mind after the weekend. Most of my readers were writer friends, eager to try the exercises and share what they came up with. I think many began to look forward to Mondays because they automatically had something they could post on their own blogs that day: their response to the writing prompt! Other readers would see their posts, as well as the link to where it came from, and join in the fun. We'd leave comments for each other, sharing what phrases or moments we particularly liked. Slowly, a strong and supportive community formed and grew, and I've been doing this ever since.

Posting prompts on Monday mornings forces me into a state of thoughtfulness. I ask myself, What can I give to my writer friends today? What can I share that will inspire them to also go into a state of thoughtfulness, the place we writers need to be in order to create meaningful work? I think that often, when we start the week by writing something for the pure joy and practice of it, we discover the beauty and depth of meaning in our surroundings in a way that makes us better observers for all of our other work. I think this is why a lot of my prompts focus on simply taking in our surroundings and telling the story of what we see. After all, every object has a story, real or imagined.

As more people learned about my prompts, teachers began to visit and to share them with their students. Sometimes they would share student writing with me in the comments. It's always a treat to see a simple idea make its way into a classroom and be interpreted in vastly different ways by students of various ages. It shows us all what unique voices we have! It's particularly fun and rewarding to see students recognize that for the first time.

When Kate asked me to participate in Teachers Write, the feature seemed like a perfect fit. Teachers from all over the world have participated and shared their work. We've made each other laugh, cry, and think more deeply. Above all, we've grown together. Sharing prompts is a very intimate practice, and it requires a level of trust among the participants. Writers need to feel safe and free to let go and push themselves to write honestly and bravely. Sometimes that involves writing about a personal experience, and sometimes it involves trying a new way of writing, such as from a different point of view. Both can be scary. But in a supportive and safe environment, pushing ourselves to go deeper and beyond our comfort zone is encouraged and celebrated, rather than something to fear. I've seen prompts I've provided evolve into poems, essays, stories, and novels. Tossing a phrase to writers and seeing what surprising places they take it has been one of the most rewarding experiences of my career.

JO'S MORNING WARM-UP

One of my favorite exercises to help people get started is to have them describe the kitchen of their childhood. If you moved around a lot, choose the one that has the strongest memories. Place your child self in that room. Now:

What do you see? Describe the room in as much detail as you can remember.

What do you smell? Was yours a kitchen of delicious odors? Or was it rarely used? What kinds of foods were cooked? Did you like them? Why or why not?

What do you hear? What kinds of conversations took place in the kitchen, if any? Were there moments of joy? Arguing? Worry? Love?

What do you taste? What are the strongest tastes you remember? A morning bowl of cereal? The batter on a spoon? Who made the food?

As you write, you will likely notice a plethora of memories flooding your brain and your heart. Seize these and write them down. Describe them in as much detail as you can. Soon, you will discover a story taking shape. Grab it!

Jo Knowles is the author of *Read Between the Lines, Living with Jackie Chan, See You at Harry's, Pearl, Jumping Off Swings,* and *Lessons from a Dead Girl*. Her awards and honors include *New York Times* and ALA Notable Book distinctions and the PEN New England Children's Book Discovery Award. Jo has a master's degree in children's literature from Simmons College. She has been a volunteer writing mentor at a Vermont women's prison and cotaught at a teen writing camp for several years. She teaches in the MFA program at Southern New Hampshire University. Visit her website at www.joknowles.com. For more of Jo's Morning Warm-Ups, go to www.joknowles.com/prompts.htm.

CHAPTER 2

Getting Started

Writing and running have a lot in common in my world. I love the idea of both. I always feel better after I've gone for a morning run or poured my thoughts onto the page, but getting started can be a challenge. Taking the first step is the hardest—whether that step involves sitting down to write or going outside to run.

In this chapter, you'll find some thoughts on how to make those first steps less painful for both you and your students.

Lesson 1, "Making Time," takes an honest look at one of the biggest barriers to writing: the twenty-four-hour limit to each day. People who write don't magically get an extra hour or two added to the day; they make time, by making choices. In this lesson, I will challenge you to examine your time to carve out space for writing each day. In the Best of Q-and-A Wednesday section that follows, you'll find tips from published authors on how to make those minutes count.

In Lesson 2, "Reading to Write," author Anne Marie Pace takes a look at the use of models and mentor texts in writing. When we study a mentor text, reading it like a writer, we're reading not only the story but also the strategies, discovering how an author created his or her work. This lesson is an important one not just for writers but for teachers of writers. Often, teachers can enlist a mentor text to instruct alongside them, providing a model for students tackling a new project or genre.

You've probably heard writers talk about their notebooks before, but just what does a writer's notebook look like? In Lesson 3, "Keeping a Writer's Notebook," I will open up a few of my notebooks to show scribbles that became the seeds for books such as *Hide and Seek* and *Eye of the Storm*. If you teach, and you keep a writer's notebook, your students will not only hear you talk about living a writing life but see you living that life as well.

Author Donna Gephart joins us for Lesson 4, "Nurturing Creativity." People who write, or make any kind of art, practice certain habits that involve writing or drawing as well as making time to notice things. Donna will share a short reading list to help nurture creativity and a super-quick writing prompt to encourage playful thinking.

If you ever struggle to come up with topics for writing, the "Three-Column Brainstorming" prompt in Lesson 5 should provide a treasure trove of ideas. It's one of my favorite strategies for generating new story possibilities and putting a fresh spin on favorite themes.

Lesson 6 is another idea generator. Author Jody Feldman likens the brainstorming process to "Mining Ideas from Thin Air" and encourages us to go digging for ideas in dreams as well as in everyday life. Learning to be inspired by random ideas is a key to regular writing.

Fear can also create a roadblock to writing, and it's a tough one to circumvent. We wonder, *What if my story/poem/book/article isn't good enough? What if people read it and don't like it? What if no one reads it at all?* The voice that whispers such questions lives somewhere inside most writers or at least pays a visit from time to time. Lesson 7, "Writing Scared," shines a light on writers' fear of failure, and though it fails to solve the problem (wouldn't that have been great?), it should inspire you to take a look at your own fears as a writer and begin to work through them. Here are some common examples of the mental roadblocks that writers face:

I'm afraid I'll fail.

I don't have any ideas.

I just don't have time.

If you want to write, that goal trumps all the reasons for not writing. And if you work with students of writing, there are even more reasons to get started.

"Writing has always been something I have wanted to do more, but I never afforded myself the time, citing how busy I was with students, teachers, and other professional responsibilities," literature coach Jenn Felt confessed after one of our summer Teachers Write sessions. "Teachers Write helped me realize that writing *is* my professional responsibility. It's kind of like that commercial with the catchphrase 'I'm not a doctor, but I play one on TV.' Before Teachers Write this summer, I think I was 'playing a writer' in school. I wrote when it was necessary to demonstrate a point in my lessons, but *living* as a writer is so much better!"

Ready to live as a writer? Go on, now . . . Get started.

Write.

JO'S MORNING WARM-UP

Go find the messiest drawer in your house. Maybe you have a designated "junk drawer" like I do, or maybe the messiest drawer in your house is your underwear drawer. If you're at work, look in your messiest drawer there. Root around and find an object that speaks to you. Does it have a funny story? A sad one? One that makes your heart skip a beat? Hold the object in your hand and close your eyes. Remember its story. Then, start writing. Make a list, write a poem, start a story. Go where the object takes you. Have fun, and be brave.

Jo Knowles is the author of *Read Between the Lines, Living with Jackie Chan, See You at Harry's, Pearl, Jumping Off Swings,* and *Lessons from a Dead Girl*. For more of her Morning Warm-Up prompts, visit www.joknowles.com/prompts.htm.

Lesson 1: Making Time

By Kate Messner

"How do you find time to write?"

For the first five years of my writing career, I was also teaching middle school full-time. I have a family, too, and people asked how I managed to write books with everything else going on. The answer is easy . . . and not so easy. I made time because it was important to me.

Nobody gets more than twenty-four hours in a day, and though some people can get by on less sleep than others, we're all on a fairly level playing field when it comes to time. Notice that the title of this lesson isn't "Finding Time." It's "*Making* Time." You can't decide that you want to write and then simply conjure up two new hours a day. Your days, like mine, are probably already full from the time you wake up until the time you go to sleep.

So where does that writing time come from? You have to *not* do something that you're currently doing, and use that time to write. Take a look at how you spend a typical day, and if you really want to write, choose something that can go. If you watch television, maybe that means not watching. Or watching half an hour less. Maybe it means checking your email once in the morning and once in the afternoon instead of flittering in and out of it all day long. Maybe it means waking up half an hour earlier, or staying up half an hour later. During the school year, maybe it means having your lunch in front of your computer or notebook instead of in the faculty room. Or maybe you can write instead of chatting with the other parents while your kid is at ballet/karate/baseball/basket-weaving practice. I don't recommend stealing time from exercise or family dinners, but there are many other options.

I do Skype author Q and A with classrooms, and not long ago, a student asked me how long it took me to write my first novel.

"Well . . . er . . . seven years," I answered a little sheepishly. There were good reasons why it took so long: I was learning my craft and had a long way to go before my work would be ready to send out. It was historical fiction and involved lots of research. I rewrote—a lot.

But there were also some not-so-good reasons. Back then, I had this idea that I needed the perfect time to write. The house had to be quiet, maybe on a day when my husband would take charge of activities with both kids. Or I needed to be away somewhere, with large open stretches of time and no ringing phone. Perfect quiet. Throw in a cupcake or two while you're at it. And if all those conditions weren't met? Well, never mind then. I'll never get anything done, so I might as well not bother trying.

Since then, I've learned that the myth of perfect writing time is just that, a myth. Sure, those ideal situations happen—usually twice a year for me, in the form of a couple of retreats that I attend. But you don't get books written in eight days a year. You get books written by writing regularly, whether the conditions are perfect or not. And you learn to write some pretty good stuff with noise. And without cupcakes.

It really comes down to this. If you want to write, you need to do these things:

- Look at how you spend your time now. What can go?
- Make time. Fifteen or twenty minutes a day is a great start. Make it an appointment with yourself, and then keep it.
- Make space. If you choose a place to write, as well as a time, you'll be more likely to stick to your routine. It doesn't have to be fancy—one of my friends set up a tiny desk in her closet—but it helps to have a place where you usually write.
- Share your plans with the other people who live in your house, and remind them that this is important to you.

TODAY'S ASSIGNMENT

Make a writing plan for the next two weeks.

If you're having trouble making time, start with a close look at how you currently spend your time. Then write for a while in response to these questions:

- How many hours per week do you spend watching television? Online? Sleeping? Talking on the phone?
- What have you found that you might be able to cut out of your schedule or cut back on to make time to write?
- During the next two weeks, when will you be writing each day, and for how long? Remember to be realistic. Fifteen minutes is fine to start.
- Where will you usually write? This can be different places on different days, depending on your schedule.
- Now, tell someone about your plans, whether that's your writing group or your family or a friend. Remember, sharing your writing plans with the people in your life helps to make them real and reminds your family and friends to give you that space for writing.

Lesson 2: Reading to Write

By Anne Marie Pace

One day, when my oldest daughter was about nine, she handed me a sheaf of papers with a story scrawled across the pages and asked me to read it. As I read, I started chuckling. In her story, my daughter had unconsciously mimicked the books in Ann M. Martin's Baby-Sitters' Club Little Sisters series. The characters' names and situations were different, but the pacing, style, and voice were spot-on. It made perfect sense. She had devoured the series, reading the books again and again. Of course, that voice poured out when she began to write.

LEARNING TO SPEAK, LEARNING TO WRITE

We learn spoken language through immersion. Babies are born unable to speak, but within a relatively brief time, most can ask for juice and name their body parts. Learning to write is somewhat more complicated, of course, but few would dispute that most avid readers find writing easier than those who read less. You've probably observed this in your students.

In fact, new writers are sometimes counseled to read one thousand books in the genre they wish to write in before they start to write. Chances are good that you write in a certain format or genre because you enjoy reading it. If you've read enough, the basic conventions of the genre may come easily to you. But learning by osmosis takes you only so far. You can't just read the thousand books and hope for the best; you have to pay attention to what you read. If you want to write with more effective craft than just the bits and pieces you've picked up along the way, you have to study good writing and figure out just how authors do what they do.

WHY WE USE MODELS

Teachers use models with students all the time, whether it's a model essay or research paper in English class, a model lab report in biology, or a model still life in art.

Why do we do this for our students? Sometimes, the model simply sets an expectation: this is what you should include in your lab report. Sometimes, it's freeing. Writing poetry to some predetermined structure (say, modeling an apology poem on William Carlos Williams's "This Is Just to Say") means you don't have to think about structure. That part is done for you, so you have more time to think about ideas, themes, or word choice. Sometimes, studying a model is empowering. Breaking the writing down into manageable chunks makes a daunting larger task seem possible.

What's true for our students is true for writers as well. Studying models sets expectations: this is the quality of writing I want to aim for. It's freeing: I know from my study that chapter books of the kind I'd like to write tend to be about ten thousand words, so I will write in a style that allows me to tell a fully developed story in that number of words. And it's empowering: writing a novel is a huge task, and I don't know how to do it, but I can learn, one step at a time, from studying the best.

HOW TO USE MODELS

If this were a longer lesson, I'd want to spend some time at this point talking about using models at the macro-level or story level, the big picture. However, this isn't a weeklong workshop, so if you would like more on this, I'll recommend two books: *Hooked* by Les Edgerton and Ann Whitford Paul's *Writing Picture Books*. Both make excellent use of models in their discussion.

What I'd like to do instead is give you some examples of reading-to-write along my own writing journey, in hopes that they might inspire you to do something similar, in whatever way they might work for you.

In 2003, I decided to recast a short story I'd written into a middle grade novel. I had the plot, characters, setting, and so on already laid out (in short story form), but I was having trouble beginning. So I filled in this sentence: *The readers who will like my work probably liked ________________ and ________________.*

In this case, the answer to one of those blanks was Patricia MacLachlan's *Sarah, Plain and Tall*. (Yes, a collective sigh at its glory is appropriate here.) I pulled it off the shelf and began to take notes.

> *Chapter 1: 10 short pages; around 200 words per page; total for chapter around 1,400 words*
>
> *Introduces immediately that Mama is gone, that novel is set in the past (fire), time of day, dogs. "Did Mama sing every day?" asked Caleb. 2nd paragraph–that years have passed since Mama died, that Anna has been "raising" Caleb and is somewhat tired of it. Sets up that Papa has changed. A few sensory details fill in. Interesting that they are sound details, maybe to replace the missing song–but they are not beautiful sounds, a "hollow scraping sound," the crackling of a log breaking apart.*

Humor–Caleb looks like bread dough with hair.

Worst thing about Caleb takes her into memory of Mama's death, which takes her to description of setting and how now it's winter but it has seemed like winter since Mama died.

Caleb brings her back to the present, talks more about Mama. She starts to cry but Papa comes in.

Life continues, with small brief details. Then Caleb asks Papa about singing–Papa says he's forgotten but here's a way to remember–tells about Sarah. Sarah's letter is brief, poignant, more literary than factual.

End of chapter loops back to the singing. "Ask her if she sings, I said."

Some notes were directly helpful, and others were less so. But as I thought about *Sarah's* first chapter, two points stood out: the importance of sensory detail and how MacLachlan picked them to highlight Caleb's and Anna's emotions, and the looping from the first sentence to the last, with the motif threaded in (in this case, singing). When I began to write, this is what came to me:

The scents of ginger and molasses curl around me like a patchwork quilt, warming the kitchen in the way that only the smell of baking cookies can do.

I can't help remembering how ginger cookies are Billy's favorite, how he had a sixth sense about them. Even if he was working way up the hill, he would manage to bound into the kitchen as soon as the first batch was pulled from the oven. He would eat half the tray in one fell swoop, until Mama slapped his hand away and told him to save a few for Christmas Day. But as I open my mouth to say so, I see the tightness of Mama's lips and her tired eyes and know she is already remembering the same thing. I shut my mouth again, drawing the thought back inside me tightly.

Billy isn't here this year. He isn't here now, and he won't be here for Christmas, and he won't be here in the New Year. And maybe never.

Mama wraps a towel around her hand and reaches into the oven to pull the tin baking sheet from the oven. She bangs it on the table to loosen the cookies, a little harder than maybe it needs to be banged. I wonder if she's wishing she hadn't baked ginger cookies at all.

But maybe she's hoping like I am—hoping that, wherever Billy is, the smell of ginger cookies will drift like smoke just as far as he has drifted, will seek him out and tap him on the shoulder, as if he were just up on the ridge, and lead him back to our kitchen. And he'll follow that smell to the railroad track, he'll swing onto a passing car, and he'll ride the rails back to Gordonsville, he'll hitch a ride as farther more along as he can hitch, he'll make the rest of the way on foot up the road and into the hollow.

He'll find his cookies waiting, and find me waiting, too.

That exercise helped me shape that passage, which at the time I thought was a first chapter (after many revisions; it's now just a section in the middle of the manuscript). But I also used my notes on a smaller level. Take a look at these lines from *Sarah.*

"Well, Papa doesn't sing anymore," said Caleb very softly. A log broke apart and crackled in the fireplace.

In simple terms, it's dialogue followed by a bit of scene setting. To me, it has more depth; that particular image of the breaking log emphasizes the brokenness of Anna's and Caleb's family because of their mother's death. If it were just a question of word count or pacing, MacLachlan could have used a whistling teakettle or a flickering light or Papa's stomping boots outside to fill in that spot, but she didn't; she chose a breaking log. Now, I have absolutely no idea if that choice was intentional or if I'm reading something into it that MacLachlan didn't intend. For our purposes, that doesn't matter. What I learn from this bit is that I can make conscious choices about my words to give them deeper meaning. Thus I chose to have my main character imagine the scent of baking cookies drifting outside and even across the country, mirroring her brother's journey.

TODAY'S ASSIGNMENT

Fill in the blank: The readers who will like my work probably like __________ .

Study the opening section or chapter of whatever work you used to fill in that blank. What about that work do you think readers respond to? Why does it work so well? What reaction does it evoke in you? How? What specific techniques does the author use to make it work? How can you apply what you have learned to your own writing?

Now, take a paragraph from your work in progress. Use your answers to the previous questions to help you revise it into a stronger, more effective piece of writing.

Anne Marie Pace is proud to be part of an extended family full of educators, all the way back to her great-grandfather, who taught in a one-room schoolhouse, and including both parents, her husband, her sister, and her sister's husband. Anne Marie taught middle and high school English in Virginia for five years before leaving teaching to raise her four children and write full-time. She is the author of several picture books from Scholastic Reading Clubs and Disney-Hyperion, most notably the Vampirina Ballerina series, illustrated by LeUyen Pham. Visit her website at www.annemariepace.com.

Lesson 3: Keeping a Writer's Notebook

By Kate Messner

When people ask me about how to get started writing, I almost always share the same two pieces of advice, whether those people are nine years old, or thirty-five, or seventy.

The first thing is this: Read. Readers develop an ear for what good sentences sound like and a sense for what makes a story work. Reading will make you a better writer.

The second piece of advice is this: Write. This may sound ridiculous, but you'd be surprised how many people talk about wanting to write without actually sitting down and doing it. A writer's notebook is a good way to start.

There are some very strict rules for having a writer's notebook. Here they are:

Rule 1: Write in it.

Rule 2: There are no other rules.

A writer's notebook can have a million different jobs. Some people scribble a few lines first thing every morning when they wake up. Some write throughout the day, at breakfast, in the grocery checkout line, waiting for the kids to get out of school. You can use a writer's notebook to journal, to scribble story ideas, to record snatches of conversation or names you like or the way the leaves make swishing sounds in the wind. You get the idea.

So if you don't already have one, choose a notebook. And write things in it. Here are some of my notebooks (Figure 2.1).

FIGURE 2.1
Writer's notebooks

I am a multiple-notebook kind of writer. I usually have at least three going at once. The little black ones are "idea books," and every time I get a new book idea while I'm working on a project, I scribble a note on one page—it gets only a page—and then I go back to my work in progress. These idea books are where I go sniffing around for stories when I'm ready to start something new.

I have a shameless addiction to Ecojot notebooks, and I often have a big one that I'm using for taking research notes on whatever book I'm working on as well as a small one that I carry around for all sorts of scribbles. The thing about my writer's notebooks is this: They aren't sacred. They are full of all kinds of things, often all mixed together.

Figure 2.2 shows a page where I was brainstorming ideas for *Hide and Seek*, my mystery set in the rain forest of Costa Rica.

FIGURE 2.2
Notebook brainstorming for *Hide and Seek*

Figure 2.3 shows a list of questions I wanted to remember to ask one of the tornado specialists whom I interviewed in Oklahoma when I was researching my weather thriller, *Eye of the Storm.*

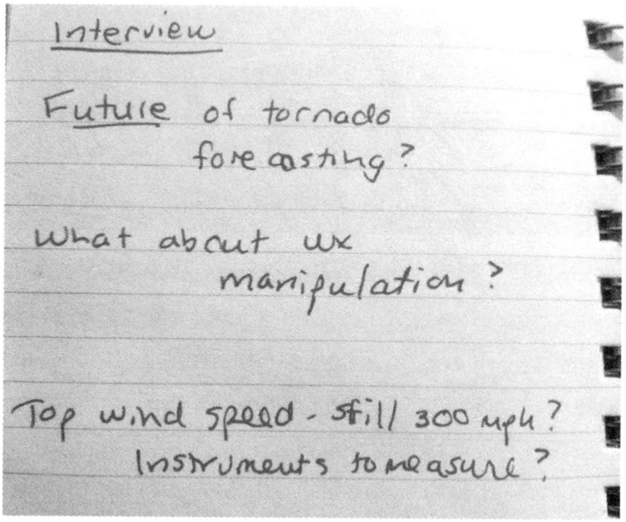

FIGURE 2.3
***Eye of the Storm* research questions**

In Figure 2.4, you will see a page I scribbled when I was outside one spring day, writing with my seventh-grade students. We were practicing noticing details.

FIGURE 2.4
Notebook observations

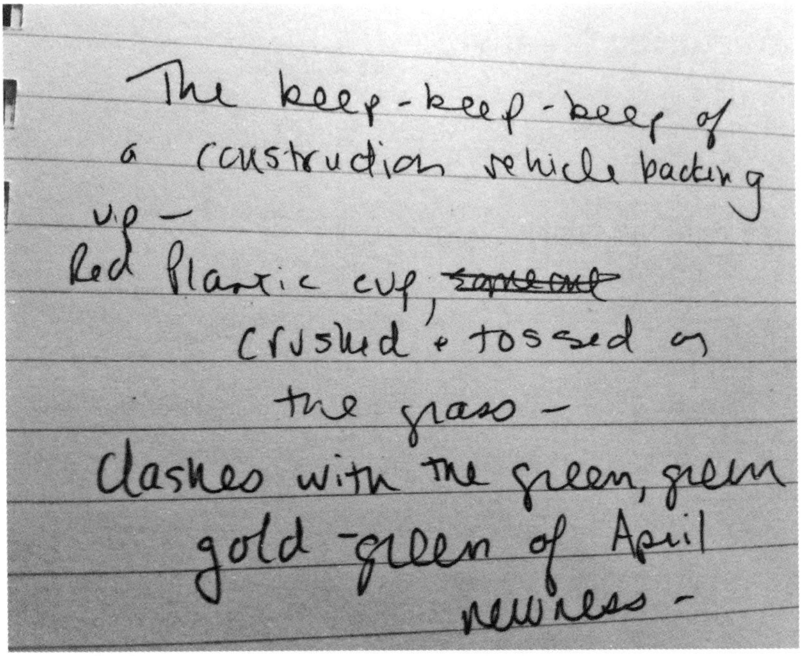

My notebooks are full of entries similar to these, as well as collections of names, descriptions of clothes I borrowed from strangers to save for my characters later on, blurted "what-ifs" that I scribbled because I thought they might help solve story problems, and funny things my kids and their friends said, all mixed in with a scattering of to-do lists, grocery lists, and tic-tac-toe games from when the kids were bored waiting at the dentist's office. This eclectic mix makes for a lot of searching when I need to find something, but the whole mishmash also creates a fertile breeding ground for fresh ideas. The process works for me. You'll figure out what works best for you.

Your writer's notebook doesn't have to be perfect or sacred. It doesn't have to be tidy. It should be something you reach for often, something that hangs out with you so much, you will feel naked if you've left home without it. Practice having it and using it. Practice writing.

TODAY'S ASSIGNMENT

If you don't already have a writer's notebook, find one. Write something. If you need inspiration, try starting with "In my writer's notebook, I hope to . . ."

Lesson 4: Nurturing Creativity

By Donna Gephart

If you want to write, it's vital to feed and nurture your creative spirit. Here are some tips, ideas, and resources that will help you stay creative throughout the year.

1. TAKE TIME OFF TO RENEW, REFILL, AND RELAX.

Read a great book . . . or a trashy one. Kick back with a fun magazine, a comic book.

Yoga and meditation encourage the brain's alpha waves. These alpha waves are linked to relaxation and creativity.

Get outside. Walk in a park or by the beach. Paddle a kayak, ride a bike, climb a mountain.

Make something—jewelry, a bird feeder, a pie. (If you make a peach cobbler, please send it to me!)

Take time off from screens. Give your brain a break from the constant stimulation of technology. I enjoy screen-free Sundays whenever possible—no TV, computer, smartphone, and so on. On screen-free Sundays, I connect more with people, nature, and books. (And the pooches!)

2. GIVE YOURSELF PERMISSION TO FAIL.

Anne Lamott, author of the well-loved book *Bird by Bird: Some Instructions on Writing and Life,* called this initial failure crummy first drafts. (She actually uses a different adjective, but we'll go with *crummy* because *59 Reasons to Write* is a classroom-friendly book.)

Let go of that damaging mind-set of writing something perfect the first time. I don't know a single author who creates a "perfect" first draft. And if I did, I'd have to kill him (just on principle).

Nothing is written as much as it's rewritten. Get comfortable with your first efforts being messy. My friend Donald Vaughan, a successful freelance writer, once said, "I'd rather have a bad page than a blank page." Amen! It's much easier to work with a page than an empty one.

Don't compare yourself with others. You don't need to be Shakespeare or Steinbeck. Somebody already was Shakespeare and Steinbeck. You simply need to be your most authentic self. No one can write like you. No one has had the same experiences or ways of looking at those experiences.

And by the way, a "crummy first draft" does *not* indicate failure. It indicates practice and doing the work. It's merely part of the process. There's no need to be so focused on the result.

3. READ ABOUT CREATIVITY.

The Artist's Way, by Julia Cameron, is a staple on creativity. Her idea of morning pages—writing when you first wake—changed my writing output. I used to walk the dogs, exercise, eat breakfast, and check e-mail before I wrote. I squandered my best writing time!

Now? I wake and write. The number of pages I produce has jumped dramatically. The dogs still get walked, the emails still get answered, and so on; it's just that those things get done later in the day . . . or the next day. In fact, I wrote this entire essay in a creative burst first thing one morning.

4. CONNECT WITH CREATIVE PEOPLE.

Join or start a writer's group. Check out the Society of Children's Book Writers and Illustrators, which may already organize critique groups in your area.

Go to readings, concerts, dance performances, plays, ethnic celebrations, local festivals, museum exhibits, and so on.

Gather a few creative friends—artists, writers, performers—and discuss ideas while enjoying snacks and beverages.

Watch a TED Talk to become inspired. I love Elizabeth Gilbert's talk on nurturing creativity.

TODAY'S ASSIGNMENT

Sometimes, structure and limitation don't rein in creativity but allow it to expand to fill the parameters. With that in mind, have fun with this word-limiting creative writing prompt.

Have you heard of six-word memoirs? Write a six-word description of yourself. Here is an example:

Will write for food. Prefer royalties.

Six more words for you:

Have fun. Stay creative. Write on!

Donna Gephart's humorous writing has appeared on greeting cards, in national magazines, and on refrigerator magnets. Her honors include a Sid Fleischman Humor Award, and her novel *Olivia Bean, Trivia Queen*, about a *Jeopardy!*-obsessed twelve-year-old, received a starred Kirkus review. See more at www.donnagephart.com.

Lesson 5: Three-Column Brainstorming

By Kate Messner

As a reader, I've discovered that some of my favorite books have wonderful elements of the unexpected: familiar characters in unexpected settings, for instance, or traditional plotlines with unexpected twists.

As a writer, I've learned that the first idea I come up with for a new story might not be the most original one, so I've developed a three-column brainstorming strategy that helps me think outside the box and combine ideas in unexpected ways.

In the first column, I make a list of things I love, things that fascinate me, and things that scare me. All of these ideas can be great story starters. The ideas might be random and unrelated; those on a recent list included everything from ghosts to volcanoes to venomous snakes.

In the second column, I make a list of settings: places I know and love, places that fascinate or intrigue me, places I'd like to visit, and places I wish were real. Again, these are wildly diverse—the Everglades, outer space, the circus . . . you name it.

In the third column, I make a list of possible genres, moods, and themes—big ideas I'd like to explore. Column three brainstorming might include words such as *mystery, thriller, friendship, ghost stories, secrets, humor,* and more. Figure 2.5 shows a sample brainstorming chart.

FIGURE 2.5
Sample brainstorming chart

STUFF I LIKE/FIND INTERESTING	PLACES I LOVE/WANT TO VISIT	GENRES/MOODS/THEMES
Sea monsters	The bridge behind my house	Ghost story
Concussions	Costa Rica	Mystery
Tornadoes	The future	Friendship
Jazz band	Outer space	Questions
Snakes	The desert	Humor
Dreams	Paris	Thriller
Revolutionary War	Airports	Creepy
Chocolate	Everglades	Fantasy/magic
Hedgehogs	Doctor's office	Wanting a pet

Next comes the fun part. I take an idea from column one and try it out with different settings and themes. Let's use ghosts as an example. The traditional ghost story is set in a haunted house, but what if we played around with the setting? What might a ghost do at an amusement park or a soccer game? What if we took that ghost to school or to outer space? Then, we'd look at the third column and consider how a ghost story might also include humor, or ideas on the theme of friendship or secrets. Suddenly, a single idea, ghosts, has almost infinite possibilities.

TODAY'S ASSIGNMENT

Make your own three-column brainstorming chart. Then, choose an idea from the first column and play around with possible settings, genres, and themes. Which ideas rise to the surface?

Lesson 6: Mining Ideas from Thin Air

By Jody Feldman

When I was a kid, I originally concluded that I was incapable of Important Thoughts. Being naturally competitive, I didn't let my internal conversation stop there. I learned how to mine ideas from what often seems to be thin air.

The process is as simple and as difficult as opening your eyes and ears and instincts, and consciously noting what's happening both around you and inside your mind. I offer four suggestions—practices I've integrated into my everyday life.

Extend your dreams. Even if it means setting your alarm several minutes early, lie in bed and hold on to that semi-sleep state. Grab an image from your mind. Assign it to a character. See what new ideas evolve while you're still hazy.

Reading a new book? Pause right in the middle of the story. How would you end it? Is your ending satisfying? Dig deeper. Think of another road to travel. Is your ending different? Try building a separate story around it.

Go to a public place. Observe. Watch that guy use a tissue after he sneezes. Imagine, instead, if he wiped his nose on his sleeve. On his bare arm. On a napkin from his lunch mate's tray. What if he sneezed out fire? Or was propelled upward? Let your mind run with the possibilities.

Get in touch with your mini adrenaline rushes. What makes your ears perk up? What raises your creative antennae? Go to any bookshelf and look at the titles. Which words stir your insides, have you wondering about the story? Visit any museum—art, history, science. What objects stop you? Make you take a second look? Follow those thoughts.

TODAY'S ASSIGNMENT

Get inspired by a single word. Go to the random noun generator:
www.wordgenerator.net/noun-generator.php.
The first word that pops up is yours for the day. You have two choices:

Brainstorm—Generate a full page of plot ideas with that noun at the center of your thoughts. Need a boost? Add a second word.

Dive in—Let your noun kick-start a piece of writing. The word generator, for example, gave me *expansion*. My first, raw thought:

Whenever Parker caught sight of the Four Springs Expansion Bridge, he always gasped a little.

Funny. Now I want to know why.

Jody Feldman blames her seventh-grade English teacher (justly or not) for turning her away from writing, yet the world mysteriously led her back. She is the author of *The Seventh Level* and *The Gollywhopper Games* and sequels. Visit her website at www.jodyfeldman.com.

Lesson 7: Writing Scared

By Kate Messner

It's impossible to be a new writer without feeling flashes of fear, worry that the work won't be good enough or that we have no business writing at all. This is where you're probably expecting me to say, "Don't be afraid" or "There's no reason to be scared." But I'm not going to say that.

Be scared. That's absolutely fine. Because you know what? I'm scared, too, every time I start a new book. When I was writing my first book, I thought this would be a temporary thing, that the second and third books would be easy and fun and fearless. But no. Turns out they're all scary in different ways, and making art is inherently fear producing. There's a whole book about this idea, by the way, *Art and Fear* by David Bayles and Ted Orland. It's an excellent read and shows us why making art is scary in a *good* way.

You see, there are two kinds of fear. The first kind keeps you safe from things that might cause you real and imminent harm.

My son and I encountered this cottonmouth (see Figure 2.6) while we were hiking in the Everglades a few years ago. We were scared, and we quickly identified our fear as the kind that saves you from danger. With this kind of fear, it's good and healthy to act and run away to avoid venomous bites and other potentially fatal things.

FIGURE 2.6
Cottonmouth snake

But there's another kind of fear—the kind that we feel when we're about to exceed the artificial limits we've set for ourselves. When we're about to step outside of our cozy little boxes and try something new. Something that's scary because we might fail. And what will people think?

I learned a lot about this second kind of fear in March 2012, when I gave a TED Talk at the organization's annual conference in Long Beach. There were fifteen hundred people in the audience, including CEOs of huge companies, inventors, producers, engineers, a former vice president, and other leaders in just about every area imaginable. One of the other speakers was Bill Nye the Science Guy, who said something that I am going to remember for the rest of my life. He told one of the other anxious speakers, "If you weren't nervous, it wouldn't be worth doing." And he was right. I was terrified when I stepped onto that stage. Absolutely terrified. It was extremely uncomfortable. But I learned so much from the experience, and I wouldn't trade it for anything.

The kind of fear I was feeling is not the kind we should avoid. It's the kind we should seek, because it gives us opportunities to be brave and grow. In fact, during our first summer of our Teachers Write camp, writer-teacher Colby Sharp reminded me of a line from Linda Urban's wonderful novel *Hound Dog True*: "You can't have brave without scared." It's true.

The twist of anxiety you feel about sharing your writing? Think of it as a big, huge billboard in your heart that says, "GO, YOU!! YOU ARE DOING SOMETHING AWESOME AND NEW!" And after you do the new awesome thing, you will never be quite the same. Your world will be a little bigger. And this is good.

So go on now. Be scared. Be brave. And write.

TODAY'S ASSIGNMENT

Often, naming our fears and bringing them out in the open makes them feel less daunting. So spend a few minutes reflecting on this prompt:

Sometimes, writing scares me because . . .

Q+A - THE BEST OF Q-AND-A WEDNESDAY: MAKING TIME

Sometimes, we talk about "finding" time to write, as if we might check under the sofa and come up with an extra hour or two. In reality, there is no *finding* time—only *making* time. Our guest authors share some strategies and schedules that work for them.

QUESTION: I love to write—I've always been a writer—but my issue seems to be making that dedicated time to write each day. It's so difficult for me to do with young kids. Any tips?

ANSWERS:

It is really hard to find time every day when you have small kids. When my three were little, I wrote at whatever odd times I could (nap time, early morning, after they'd gone to bed). But don't be too hard on yourself if you can't carve out the same block of time every day. However, it's great to get into the habit now, while they're young, of carving out an hour here or there as often as you can, and not *doing the dishes or folding laundry. Give yourself permission to use the time writing. Better yet, splurge on a babysitter from time to time. It will get ever so slightly easier as they get older (but I still do a lot of writing in weird places, like in the [parked] car or sitting in bleacher seats!).*

~Sarah Albee, author of *Poop Happened: A History of the World from the Bottom Up* and *Bugged: How Insects Changed History*

I love *Sarah's answer. And I always carry a notebook in my pocket–it's been invaluable!*

~Lynda Mullaly Hunt, author of *One for the Murphys* and *Fish in a Tree*

I can remember writing the first draft of Goldie Locks Has Chicken Pox *in the pickup line at my daughter's elementary school, on three different kinds of paper (whatever was in the car or my purse) and four colors of ink and pencil. I found myself revising aloud while in the shower–my only alone time. I like the idea of giving yourself permission to hire a babysitter to allow writing time. I'm a firm believer in showing our kids how parents follow their dreams.*

~Erin Dealey, author of *Deck the Walls*

Q+A - THE BEST OF Q-AND-A WEDNESDAY: INTIMIDATED BY GREAT WRITING

If reading great writing sometimes makes you feel insecure about your own work, you're far from alone. Writer-teacher Colby Sharp asked guest authors to chime in on this subject during our summertime Teachers Write camp:

QUESTION: Yesterday I read through some of the responses people had shared via Teachers Write, and I thought to myself, Man, all this amazing writing makes me feel like a loser and incompetent. I was wondering if any authors ever felt like that when they read published books or other writing.

ANSWERS:

When you read the writing of others, it's easy to get intimidated. (Imagine how our students feel!) The thing to keep in mind is that you have a unique voice and perspective as well. No one writes like you do. No one can tell the stories in your heart the way you would. If all artists painted exactly like Van Gogh or Picasso, where would they be?

I realized long ago that my writing does not fall into the "literary" category. You don't have to write incredible prose to consider yourself a writer. Give yourself permission to be your own unique storyteller and see what happens.

~Erin Dealey, author of *Deck the Walls*

All. the. time.

Example: yesterday, reading Wonder.

~Gae Polisner, author of *The Pull of Gravity* and *The Summer of Letting Go*

It is very easy to feel intimidated by someone else's powerful writing. You can short-circuit that insecurity by turning it into inspiration: What does this writer do that you admire? What can you take from your experience with this book? I see sporting events and live comedy, and I listen to my favorite bands. I can't do any of that stuff, but seeing others push themselves to achieve their goals or watching the way a comedian or singer uses words and rhythm to move people is something I take with me into my writing.

~Danette Haworth, author of *A Whole Lot of Lucky* and *Violet Raines Almost Got Struck by Lightning*

I have to agree with the others. A few years ago, at a writing retreat, the speakers provided writing prompts for us, and many of the attendees shared their writing. I was in awe that they could create such interesting, amazing writing "on the fly." My first thought was I shouldn't be here. There is no way I can write prose that polished in the few minutes we were given. *But after some deeper reflection, I realized that I'm much more of a rewriter than I am a writer. And that's okay. We all have our own processes and our own strengths and weaknesses. Hope this helps!*

–Katy Duffield, author of *Farmer McPeepers and His Missing Milk Cows* and *California History for Kids: Missions, Miners, and Moviemakers*

I feel this way all the time, Colby. (In fact, I have a shelf in my writing room that's reserved for books I wish I'd written.) But the trick is to let that work inspire rather than intimidate you. And remember, you have something that no one else in the universe has . . . not me or Linda Urban or Jenni Holm or Jack Gantos or anyone else. You have Colby Sharp's voice. Let it shine.

–Kate Messner, author of *All the Answers, How to Read a Story,* and the Silver Jaguar Society Mysteries

CHAPTER 3

Organizing

It's time for a confession. Through most of my school years, I was one of those kids who did the writing first, then backtracked to complete the required outline so that I could collect my extra five points. Fast-forward to the present, where I earn my living as a full-time writer, and sometimes, I still write first and outline later. These days, though, it's not about points or credit but about using outlines as a revision tool.

Ask a hundred published writers how they organize their ideas, and you're likely to get a hundred different answers. Some authors outline each scene meticulously before they begin to write. Some scratch out just a few rough ideas and then plow ahead to draft an entire novel. Some draw. Some build time lines or maps or idea webs. And some write by the seats of their pants and never think about organization until a first draft is complete and it's time to go back to revise. But all of these writers address organization eventually, in many different ways. Whether you're an early outliner or a writer who drafts in the dark, you'll find plenty of ideas for how to organize your thoughts in this chapter.

Lesson 8, "Creating the Tools We Need," is especially for writers who never fell in love with prefabricated idea webs and graphic organizers. I'll share some examples from my own writing life—the mystery web that guides my plotting when I'm writing a whodunit and the ever-useful "Eats/Gets Eaten By" chart I made to get a better sense for how particular animals in the Costa Rica rain forest are interconnected. Sometimes, the very best tool for organizing your writing is one that you invent to match that particular piece of writing.

Author Sally Wilkins is a fan of more traditional outlines. In Lesson 9, "Outlining: When, Why, and How," she shares how she uses outlines to guide her writing.

In Lesson 10, "Talking About Time," author Linda Urban takes a look at the importance of tracking time in a story and offers suggestions for how writers might manipulate those hours and minutes. Not every moment in a story has equal importance. Some deserve more weight, more time, than others. This lesson shares strategies that allow writers to "fast-forward" from important moment to important moment and ideas for slowing the clock as well—"stopping time" to explore those moments that matter most.

Different kinds of writing require different kinds of planning. Works of futuristic fiction, science fiction, and fantasy—really, any stories that don't take place in our already-established world—require a special kind of organization. In Lesson 11, "World Building," author Mike Jung introduces writers to this concept and shares some thoughts on how writers might create consistent, believable worlds.

Lesson 12, "Futuristic World-Building Worksheet," connects world building to futuristic fiction. I share the detailed world-building worksheet I created when I was working on my futuristic weather thriller, *Eye of the Storm*. The set of questions can be used to generate details for virtually any fictional futuristic world.

Wherever you make use of these lessons in your writing process, as prewriting activities or revision tools, you'll find that there are as many ways to organize a story as there are kinds of writers.

JO'S MORNING WARM-UP

Draw a map of the home you grew up in. As you map things out, try to note specific memories you associate with a certain room or special spot outside. Like the time you crashed your bike in the driveway. Or where your cat (what was her name?) used to sun herself. Include as many details as you can possibly fit. You'll be amazed at the memories that start to surface once you get going.

Jo Knowles is the author of *Read Between the Lines, Living with Jackie Chan, See You at Harry's, Pearl, Jumping Off Swings,* and *Lessons from a Dead Girl*. For more of her Morning Warm-Up prompts, visit www.joknowles.com/prompts.htm.

Lesson 8: Creating the Tools We Need

By Kate Messner

Not all writers work well with traditional outlines, and not all writing projects demand that kind of structure. Rather than imposing a canned outline or graphic organizer on a piece of writing, it's often best to create our own tools to meet the needs of the job. What might that look like?

When I started writing my first mystery, *Capture the Flag* (see Figure 3.1), I was only a few pages into the first chapter when I realized that writing without an organized plan was going to lead to a great big mess. If I couldn't keep the characters and their details straight in my own head, how was a reader going to do so? What I needed, I realized, was a one-page road map that showed the characters, their relationships to one another, and their relationships to the important objects in the story.

FIGURE 3.1
Capture the Flag

After reading some great resources on the genre (I highly recommend *Writing Mysteries*, edited by Sue Grafton, and *Now Write! Mysteries*, edited by Sherry Ellis and Laurie Lamson), I came up with a graphic organizer—an idea web to keep all my mysterious details in order.

In the center of that idea web, I put the object of the heist: the original "Star-Spangled Banner" from the Smithsonian Museum of American History. Branching out from that, I listed the suspects and all of their possible motives. (Note that in a mystery many of the "suspects" are innocent, but the writer still needs to consider the reasons they might have committed the crime.) On another branch, I explored the investigators, and I explored their motives as well. After all, most of us don't wake up in the morning looking for random crimes to investigate. The web grew as I noted the clues and false clues left by various suspects, and in the end, this 11-by-17-inch chart became my master plan for *Capture the Flag*. It also became a great tool that I use when I'm working with writing students, a road map for building a mystery.

Want to try your hand at crafting a mystery? Start with a crime, and write that at the center of your web. Next, brainstorm possible suspects and their motives, investigators and their motives, and clues that might have been left behind. From there, your plot will emerge. See Figure 3.2 for an example.

FIGURE 3.2
Sample mystery web

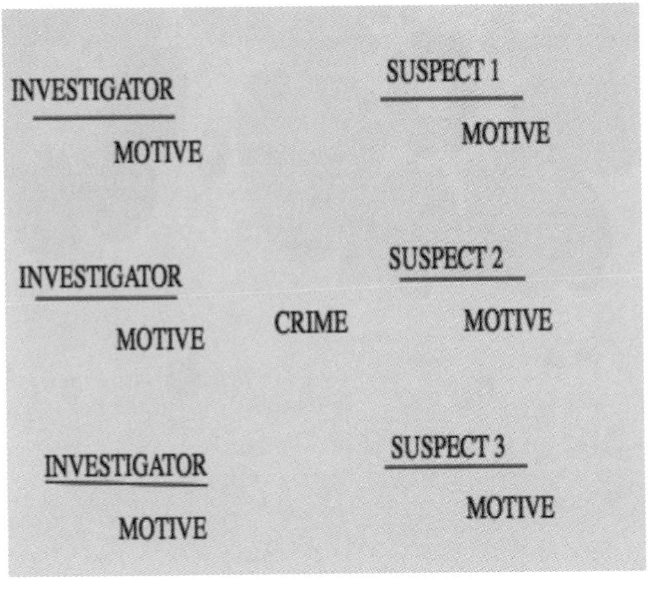

Inventing your own organizational tools is a great way to explore issues that are specific to your book. My picture book *Tree of Wonder: The Many Marvelous Lives of a Rainforest Tree* (Chronicle Books) explores the concepts of biodiversity and interconnectedness by looking at all the organisms that depend on a single species of tree in the Costa Rica rain forest. As we worked together to revise the manuscript, my editor pushed me to do more to explore those connections—not only the animals' relationships to the tree but their relationships to one another. I was struggling to organize my research notes in a way that made this clear until I developed this "Eats/Gets Eaten By" chart (see Figure 3.3).

FIGURE 3.3
Eats/Gets Eaten By chart

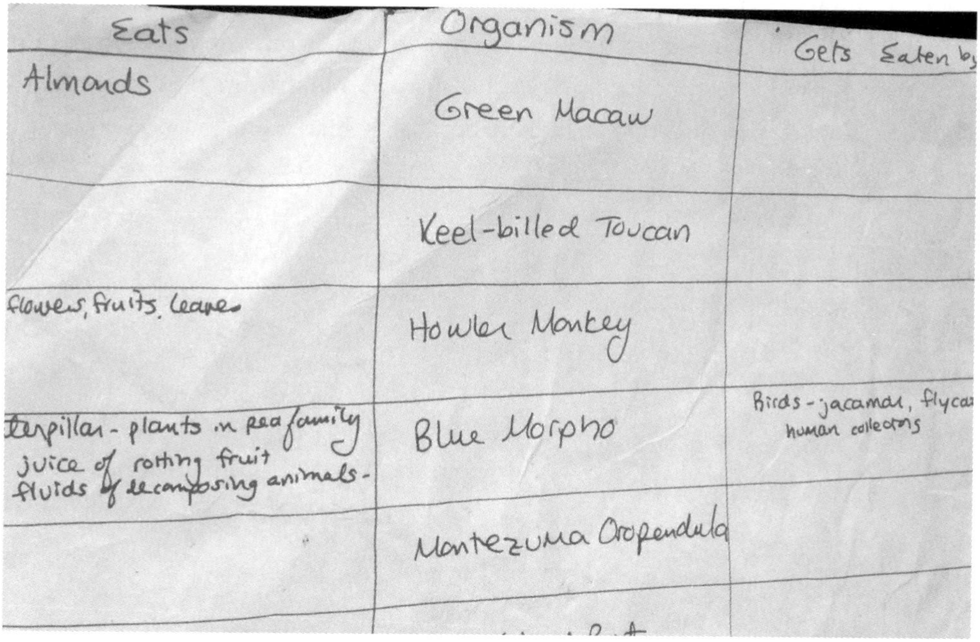
Eats
Organism
Gets Eaten by
Almonds
Green Macaw
Keel-billed Toucan
flowers, fruits, leaves
Howler Monkey
terpillar - plants in pea family
juice of rotting fruit
fluids of decomposing animals -
Blue Morpho
Birds - jacamar, flyca
human collectors
Montezuma Oropendula

On a single page, it gave me a much clearer look at those connections, and I kept that page beside my computer as I worked on a new draft of the book.

TODAY'S ASSIGNMENT
What issues and relationships will be important in your work in progress? Spend a little time brainstorming, and see if you can come up with some possible tools to help you organize the most important ideas and connections in your project.

Lesson 9: Outlining: When, Why, and How

By Sally Wilkins

We've probably all heard that writers should create outlines for their work. We know that we're supposed to be able to state the theme and summarize the plot of our books in a single sentence. We've heard expressions such as "If you don't have a map, you won't know whether you're headed toward your destination" or "Without a recipe, you're just throwing in the ingredients and hoping something edible emerges."

Most of us have felt the paralysis of trying to codify our freedom-loving creativity into that oh-so-structured outline format, and wondered, simultaneously, both *How?* and *Why?*

Some authors swear by their outlines, but others will flatly say that they don't outline. This generally means that they don't do Roman numeral/uppercase/Arabic outlines of their books or articles before they start writing. Scratch the surface of that declaration, and you'll almost certainly discover some other way they plan and organize their material—something that doesn't look or feel like an outline but works like one.

A writer's outline may take the form of a calendar or a time line. It may resemble a flowchart or, indeed, a road map (or a set of directions printed out from the Internet). For a picture book, the storyboard is a very common form of outline. Most important, a writer's outline is not a static document, created before the writer begins to write, and followed, point by point, until the end. A writer's outline is a dynamic tool. In the end, the finished work will have internalized the structure of the outline, so that a student told to make an outline of the book (especially if it is nonfiction) will be able to do just that, distilling the contents into that old familiar format. But that's the finished product!

So let's go back to the beginning and see how the writer's outline works. Every piece begins with an idea. The idea may be a theme or a topic (assigned pieces often begin this way). It may be a character, an event, or a landscape the writer wants to explore. The very first outlining that the writer does looks like jotting down notes: capturing random thoughts as they occur, adding bits and pieces of information she already knows and reminders of pieces she'll need to research or discover. The bits may include names and descriptions of characters, snatches of dialogue, one-sentence summaries of important information (with references, we hope), or photographs torn from magazines. Sometimes this jotting is an intentional, structured effort (as it will be in a classroom). Often it happens over time, frequently while the writer is working on other things, resulting in a file folder full of notes scrawled on the backs of old drafts, assorted pieces of notebook paper and stationery, and yes, envelopes and napkins.

When the writer is ready to begin the project, these random bits get grouped together—maybe by character, maybe in chronological order, maybe as stops along a journey. Although the groups may not be labeled with Roman numerals, they are, in fact, the headings of an outline. In a classroom setting, you could ask students to create that outline from the groups and bits and pieces of information, but you would need to make it clear that this is not a finished product, because it is very likely that there will be As without Bs and all kinds of other missing parts to these outlines. Give yourself that same instruction: this is a work-in-progress tool. Leave lots of blank space in each section, so you can include new material as it comes along.

This early outline not only helps you think about the structure of your writing but also highlights the places where the material is unbalanced. In a nonfiction piece, the outline will point out places where you need more research. In fiction, you'll see gaps in your narrative, characters that need developing, plot breaks where you need to construct a transition. An important observation for those who write picture books and other short form pieces: the outline may, in fact, be longer than your manuscript. The outline shown in Figure 3.4 ended up being longer than the biography for which it was created. This is the point where the "I never outline" and the "I must outline" writers generally diverge. You may choose to fill in those gaps right then, so that when you begin to write, you know every episode in your plot or every concept in your article. Or, you may trust the outline to remind you that you need to go back to them later, and begin writing with only that bare skeleton of an "outline" as a guide. Many writers don't look at it again until they complete the first draft.

As you continue to accumulate material, you'll create another kind of outline (or your original skeleton will morph into one). Building the structure of the "chapter" outline goes along with the process of mapping your work in your mind. Will it move chronologically, geographically, or thematically? How will you transition from one section or chapter to the next? For this outline your headings may be possible opening sentences, bullets, or titles. Under each heading you'll note the scene, the characters, and the action you'll be describing there. You'll note what information you'll be including and may decide some things need to be introduced earlier or held until later to improve the flow or balance of the work. When you actually begin to write, you may find yourself writing the middle of

1881 April 2. Clara Driscoll born to Robert Driscoll and Julia Fox Driscoll in St. Mary's of Aransas (near Refugio, the town was abandoned in the early 1900s).
1890 Family moves to the Palo Alto ranch, where Clara learns to ride, rope and shoot.
1898 In Spain at the outbreak of Spanish-American War, pretends to be a Spaniard for six months.
1899 Graduates from Chateau Dieudonne. Joins mother Julia and brother Robert in London where Julia dies May 23. It takes seven months to return the body to Texas, via train and steamship.
1903 Clara meets Adina de Zavala in San Antonio and joins the campaign to prevent hotel from being built on site of Alamo battle.
1906 July 31. Marries Henry (Hal) Sevier at St. Patrick Cathedral in New York City. They honeymoon three months in Italy, Paris and London.
1914 Robert Driscoll, Sr. dies. Clara and Hal return to Texas. Hal founds the *Austin American-Statesman* newspaper. They begin building Laguna Gloria.
1918-1921 On assignment with the Committee of Public Information in Buenos Aires, Argentina.
1929 Brother Bob dies. Clara and Hal move to Corpus Christi to manage the ranch and other businesses in the Driscoll empire.
1933 President Roosevelt appoints Hal as Ambassador to Chile, they move to Santiago.
1935 Hal resigns, couple returns to Texas.
1937 Clara divorces Hal and obtains court order to return to name of Driscoll.
1939 Clara pays off mortgage on Texas Federation of Women's Club building.
1940 Co-chairs and funds campaign for James Nance Garner to be Roosevelt's successor.
1942 Builds hotel with penthouse apartment on Corpus Christi Bay.
1943 Donates Laguna Gloria to Texas Fine Arts Association.
1944 Campaigns for Roosevelt's fourth term (although she had opposed the third).
1945 July 17 dies of a cerebral hemorrhage at home in Corpus Christi

FIGURE 3.4
Sample outline

the piece first, then the scene leading to the climax, circling around to fill in the blank places later. An outline allows you to do this: you don't have to write the book or article in the order that your reader will read it.

Your outlining will continue as you begin to write—the outline and the manuscript will interact, each illuminating the other. Always, the outline remains a tool, not a dictator. As you write, the work may turn in unexpected directions. New characters may show up and demand a part. A question from a critique group member may make you rethink your underlying assumptions. Write on! You can always go back and adjust the outline.

Move the pieces around. Combine some, expand others, prune and remove parts that don't work. Contrary to the oh-so-neat finished product, outlining is a messy business. Some writers like to put each section on an index card or sticky note, so they can move them around more easily.

When you have finished the first draft, do another outline, this one from the text. This outline will become a useful tool in your revisions, highlighting problem areas and enabling you to see the overall structure of your work. You can look more dispassionately at the outline/summary of each chapter and ask yourself, Is there enough action here? and Does this move the plot? With each successive draft, the outline will become tighter and cleaner. Eventually you will be able to label it "chapter synopsis" and include it in your book proposal!

Remember that outlines can take many different forms. Figure 3.5 shows one more example with story elements on a calendar.

FIGURE 3.5
Sample calendar outline

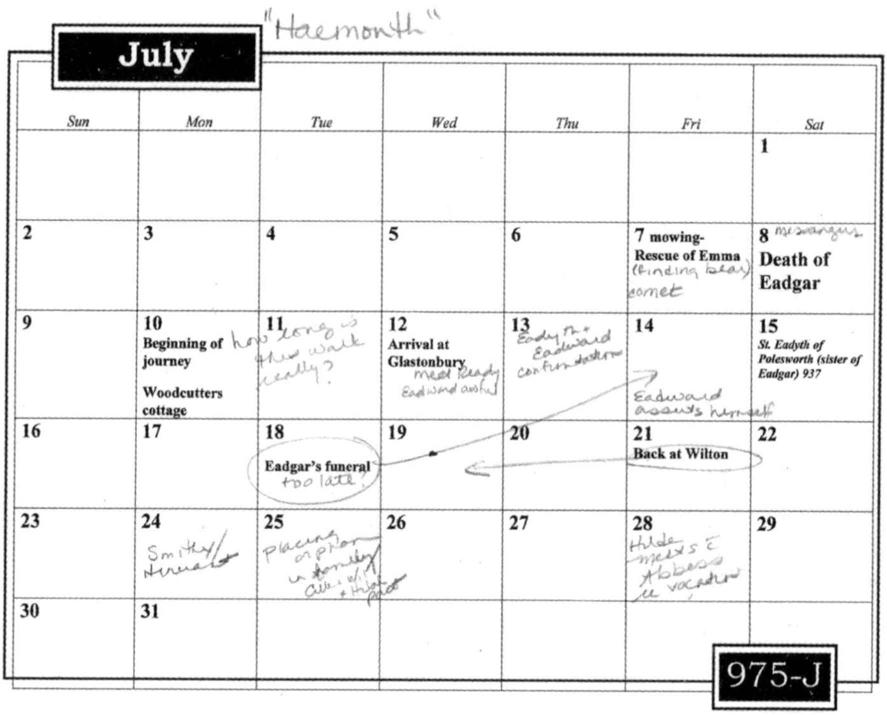

TODAY'S ASSIGNMENT

If your project is at the idea stage, start with a brain dump, jotting down all the random bits and pieces. Begin to sort them into logical groups. Create a rough outline (or time line, or map, or flowchart) from these groups.

If you already have a work-in-progress draft, create an outline from the text. Look for gaps and bulges in the outline. Think about (and jot down) how you can smooth and balance those problem areas in the next draft.

And if you don't have a work in progress but want to practice outlining and see how it all works, try creating an outline of one of your favorite books.

Sally Wilkins is a New Hampshire author and research lover who has written both nonfiction and early readers. Visit her website at www.sallywilkins.com.

Lesson 10: Talking About Time

By Linda Urban

Got a minute? Let's talk time.

One of the coolest things about writing is that we can become masters of time. We can speed it up, summarizing entire weeks of a school year in a sentence (*By the time my daily writing journal was full, I had come to the conclusion that Dana and I would never see eye to eye on this.*) or slow it down so that a second-long gesture takes on weight and importance through its extension (*Dana stared at me, her pencil tapping out a funeral march, and I swear I could see the whole history of our friendship erased in the slow, steady shake of her head.*). We use scenes to allow our readers to participate in the important stuff, to feel crucial emotions, to process information along with our characters, to experience action. We use summary to say, Here's a bit of info you'll need to know but don't have to fully engage in.

Time is one of the ways that we signal importance. We usually spend more time with major characters than minor ones. More time in scenes that detail key actions or emotions than in scenes with little consequence. You can use this assumption to your advantage. Want to hide a clue? How about sneaking it into a scene where the majority of our attention is spent on something else? Want readers to understand that a moment in a character's past shapes his or her current actions? Don't just tell us; take the time to show us in a scene.

And what about those really important parts of our story, the ones that mark crucial decisions or key turning points? We can use time to help those moments stand out in the mind of the reader.

Here's an example from my novel *The Center of Everything*, which has time (our perception of it and our desire to manipulate it) as one of its themes. In the following scene, our main character, Ruby, who has been shielding herself from her emotions after the death of her grandmother Gigi, has just seen the color-wheel project of her classmate Nero DeNiro. The wheel is creative and funny, and Ruby laughs a real, genuine laugh and *feels* for the first time in a long time. This is what happens next:

> *But when she stops laughing, all the little Nero faces start to blur. And Ruby has a bunch of thoughts.*
>
> *One of them is that there is something wrong with her eyes.*
>
> *Another is that there is something wrong with her ears, because when Lucy says, "Are you okay?" it sounds like she's using a speakerphone.*
>
> *And another is that maybe there is something wrong with her hands, because they have dropped her pencil to the floor, and even though it makes sense for her to bend over and pick the pencil up, her hands are not moving. They are just sitting there on her color wheel, covering up all the complement lines. And there are drops of water landing on her hands and on the painted squares of color, too, and the red and the orange are mixing all up into some other color that Ruby doesn't have a name for and for which there is no complement on her color wheel, and she knows she is going to get a bad grade now.*
>
> *"Ruby?" That's Mrs. Tomas talking. "Ruby? Did you hurt yourself?"*

What I hoped to do in this bit of the scene was to slow time down in terms of the way that Ruby is processing and experiencing information but also speed up the events around her. I spent time in the scene to put in the details that show how Ruby is experiencing sound, color, and movement, so that the reader can truly feel her struggling to make sense of what is happening. I cut out the details that she doesn't process, such as Lucy and Nero calling their teacher, Mrs. Tomas, over to the table to help. In playing with time in this way, I hoped to signal that this moment was unlike the ones that had come before—that it was important to Ruby and important to the story.

TODAY'S ASSIGNMENT

How might this process work in the story that you are writing? Have you come to a crucial scene yet? Is there a key moment you want your readers to slow down and really experience? Think about that moment and see if you can find one central action in it—the turning of a door handle, the connection of bat to ball, the touch of a fingertip to the nape of a neck—and slow it down. Slow it way down.

As an experiment, let's overdo the process. Let's see exactly how long we can extend this moment. Keep it moving forward but detail every sense, every thought, and every tiny change along the way. See how long you can make this moment last.

Not in the middle of a project? You can still give this process a whirl. Take a fairy tale or folktale you know well, identify a key moment, and extend it. Can you make the bite of a poisoned apple last for a paragraph? Two? A page?

When you have finished writing, take a look at what you've got. Chances are that what you've written is much longer and more detailed than anything you'd want to put into a novel or short story. But I'm betting you're going to find some great details in there, some emotions you hadn't examined before, and some key words or phrases that you'll want to keep in the scene—and maybe use again in times when you want your readers to remember that crucial plot moment.

If you did the experiment using a moment from your work in progress, put it aside for a day or two and then see if you can edit it down to something that works for you. At the very least, I'm betting that this exercise will have you thinking about that moment in a more vivid and dramatic way.

Linda Urban is the author of three novels for young readers: *A Crooked Kind of Perfect*, *Hound Dog True*, and *The Center of Everything*, which the *New York Times* called homey, funny, and "Thornton Wilderish." Her picture books are *Little Red Henry* and *Mouse Was Mad*, which was a Children's Choice Award finalist. Before turning her attention to writing, she spent ten years as marketing director for Vroman's Bookstore. Visit her website at www.lindaurbanbooks.com.

Lesson 11: World Building

By Mike Jung

Here's the Mike Jung definition of *world building*: "the process of creating the setting in which your story takes place." If you're a Tolkien fan like me, you may be recoiling in horror at the thought of creating thousands of years of history, a panoply of elfin and dwarfish peoples with their own cultures and characteristics, and a bunch of fake languages nobody can actually pronounce. But I don't think of "world building" solely as the creation of an entirely new world from the ground up, although that's certainly one option. I think of it more as creating a setting with enough credibility to evoke a sense of reality in the reader, support the suspension of disbelief you're asking of the reader, or both.

Here's an example from my own book. *Geeks, Girls, and Secret Identities* takes place in a small, contemporary city that's fairly realistic, except for the fact that it has a resident superhero, Captain Stupendous, with the powers of flight, super-strength, invulnerability, and super-vision. In fact, there are more than fifty superheroes scattered throughout the world, and they're constantly defending the safety of their respective cities by battling one crazypants supervillain or another.

Nobody's ever going to mistake my book for a work of nonfiction, and clearly readers will have to willingly engage in some suspension of disbelief. So I didn't try to create some plausible, scientifically grounded explanation of how Captain Stupendous actually could fly in the real world. There's enough pop-cultural precedent for that particular element of fantasy to make it easy to swallow.

I did, however, try to establish some consistency and logic behind the way people in the world of Geeks think and react to the thyroidal spandex-clad weirdos in their midst. For example, I created a very broadly sketched culture of superhero fandom throughout the country, a culture that's represented by two specific Captain Stupendous fan clubs in my fictional city.

I also needed to create some settings that would fill the needs of my plot, as well as the needs of my characters as real people. For example, there's this pizza parlor, which worked really well as the setting for my first chapter in terms of facilitating the plot but also fills a role in the characters' lives outside of that chapter. Kids need public places to hang out, you know? Spud's Pizza was my characters' place to hang out long before the events of the book happened. And I didn't want that because my story absolutely needed a pizza joint instead of, say, a boba teahouse, an ice cream parlor, or a convenience store full of giant-size beverages and various conglomerations of processed butter and sugar. I wanted it because it helped make my characters into people who could be real.

A character's thoughts, feelings, and actions may be driven by her pointy-eared people's fifteen millennia of dragon-infested history, but they might also be driven by the history of her local town, which has always been driven by a particular multinational company that's suddenly decided to shutter all its local facilities. A group of disenfranchised kids might end up mystically transported to a dimension that's terrorized by giant, intelligent fish, or they might face challenges with the bully population at their school, but in either case the antagonistic characters will be products of their environment and history.

All of which is a rambling way of saying that on the surface, world building is about, well, building a world: creating a sense of place, conveying specific details, establishing continuity, and making things believable, all of which are hugely important, of course. But on a deeper level, I think world building is actually a vital way of showing the history behind our stories, and ultimately, the history of our individual characters. No matter how fantastical or everyday our settings are, their ultimate purpose is to illuminate the worlds inside the hearts and minds of our characters.

TODAY'S ASSIGNMENT

Brainstorm a possible story setting that might require world building. Is it fantasy, futuristic fiction, or science fiction? What kinds of questions might you need to ask (and answer!) in order to create this fictional world?

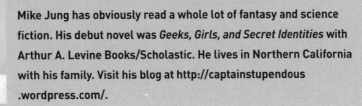

Mike Jung has obviously read a whole lot of fantasy and science fiction. His debut novel was *Geeks, Girls, and Secret Identities* with Arthur A. Levine Books/Scholastic. He lives in Northern California with his family. Visit his blog at http://captainstupendous.wordpress.com/.

Lesson 12: Futuristic World-Building Worksheet

By Kate Messner

Not all stories require the elaborate world-building methods of a fantasy, science fiction, or futuristic world, but writing in these genres does mean spending a lot of time inventing the setting before the plot can take shape. When I was beginning to think about my futuristic weather thriller, *Eye of the Storm*, I put together a world-building worksheet to help me brainstorm all the elements of that setting.

TODAY'S ASSIGNMENT

Ready to build your own futuristic world? Spend some time pondering these guiding questions, originally shared on my blog (www.katemessner.com/blog). When you're finished, take a look at the society you created and ask yourself what kind of conflict might emerge in that world. Once you've identified that, you have the makings of a great story!

Geographic location ______________________________

In the year ______________________________

In this dystopian society . . . (Write one sentence that expresses the heart of the story, the conflict as it relates to the dystopia.)

What current issue/problem is at the heart of this dystopia? From what spark of our modern reality was this world born?

____

How does the setting of this story impact the main character?

____

What are the nonnegotiable rules of this world? Are there any exceptions?

____

What laws does society impose? What happens to people who break them?

____

What rules or laws does the main character break or challenge? Why? What are the consequences?

____

What kind of government is in place? Consider local and national levels as well as international cooperation. How does the government impact citizens' everyday lives?

What official document is in place to define that government? If it is a future version of a current document (for example, the Constitution), how has it changed? What amendments have been added?

What rights do people have? What rights are they denied, and why?

What are this society's most closely held values?

What social ladders exist? Who has power, and why? What are the visible symbols of that power? Who is at the bottom of this society's social ladder, and why?

What kind of ethnic diversity exists?

What role, if any, does religion play in this society? What are the dominant religions? What religions are marginalized?

What do international/intergroup relations look like? What wars are going on? What countries or groups are fighting, and why? Which ones are allies? Which are enemies?

What climate and weather patterns are prevalent?

What does agriculture look like? Where do people get food?

What do people eat? What foods are considered common, everyday fare? What foods are delicacies, and why?

Q+A - THE BEST OF Q-AND-A WEDNESDAY: ORGANIZATION . . . AND JUMPING AROUND

QUESTION: I know there are a million ways to sketch out your story/storyboard or to outline your story before you start. I'm just wondering if any of the authors would like to talk about their particular way of doing this and share any helpful tips.

ANSWERS:

I write first and then make a story map to see where the holes are. It's called a sloppy copy for a reason. Get your idea out there first and then see where it goes. Outlining first doesn't work for me, but everyone is different.

~Erin Dealey, author of *Deck the Walls*

Some writers describe themselves as either a plotter or pantser (meaning they're writing by the seat of their pants–they aren't quite sure where a draft is going until it's finished). I'm more of a plotter. I've had some good luck with the Snowflake Method by author Randy Ingermanson. Here's a link: www.advancedfictionwriting.com/art/snowflake.php.

I've never done his entire method. I usually am ready to write before that, but it's a good way to start developing characters, setting, and plot.

But you're right–there are a million ways. The way that gets you to finish the book is the best way!

~Anne Marie Pace, author of the Vampirina Ballerina series

I love Scrivener writing software (see www.literatureandlatte.com/scrivener.php). You can download a free demo and try it out. It helped my planning/outlining so much.

~Kate Messner, author of *All the Answers, How to Read a Story,* and the Silver Jaguar Society Mysteries

QUESTION: Do you write beginning to end, or do you jump around as you are drafting?

ANSWERS:

I begin by writing the first couple of chapters, followed by the last chapter. Then I write all of the chapters in between, but in a random order. I don't plan this; the books just come to me that way. While I am making coffee in the morning, I have no idea what I will be writing that day.

When I am finished with a chapter, though, I write the chapter title on a 3-by-5-inch card and put it on a magnetic whiteboard. Then, in the coming months, as I add more chapters, I also work on putting those cards in order. It's like doing a giant puzzle!

~Lynda Mullaly Hunt, author of *One for the Murphys* and *Fish in a Tree*

I tend to be a very linear, beginning-to-end writer, but I always go back and layer stuff in–sometimes as I'm writing, other times after the first draft. But I have yet to write scenes out of order and am not sure my brain would ever allow it!

~Joanne Levy, author of *Small Medium at Large*

With my picture books, I'm a beginning-to-ender, letting the story out and then going back to edit. I smiled at [Lynda Mullaly Hunt's] mention of struggling with middles, however, because that's what happens with me–and many of my author pals on longer works.

~Erin Dealey, author of *Deck the Walls*

CHAPTER 4

Characters

We often think of character as an element of fiction, but it's just as important for writers to deliver detailed descriptions and believable personality traits for the real-life characters who inhabit research papers, biographies, and other works of nonfiction. In the early stages of writing, these characters may feel like flat, two-dimensional drawings on a page. Whether the character is a real historical figure, a living scientist, or a fictional boy wizard, it takes time, thought, revision, and often some creative strategies to bring out that character's personality. The lessons and writing prompts in this chapter take a close look at character, with some innovative brainstorming strategies and writing prompts for developing the people in your pages.

In Lesson 13, "Getting to Know Our Main Characters," guest author Jo Knowles suggests an imaginary interview. You'll sit down across from an empty chair and ask questions, then imagine the answers. When you (or your students) are writing nonfiction, some of those answers will be possible to research, but not all. Try asking an imaginary Abraham

Lincoln a question such as, "If you were alive today, what kinds of songs would be on your iPod?" An interview will prompt you to think about your character in new ways.

Guest author Jeannine Atkins invites us to stop and smell the roses—with our characters—in Lesson 14, "In the Garden." Here, we imagine characters in a specific setting, one that may not be part of the story in a work of fiction or the real-life setting in a biography or work of nonfiction. In doing so, we can consider how that character might respond to that particular world, given the challenges he or she faces.

What would Wilbur from *Charlotte's Web* share as his platform if he were running for president? What political party would support Hermione Granger or Katniss Everdeen if they were candidates for public office? In Lesson 15, "If Characters Ruled the Land," we imagine a character in the setting of a political election, which might bring out the best—or the worst—in that individual's personality.

In Lesson 16, "Studying a Character's Family," guest author Laura Wynkoop invites us into our character's childhood home to meet his or her family. We are all products of the people who raised us and grew up alongside us. This lesson lends itself beautifully to both fiction and nonfiction. Made-up characters need fully developed fictional families, whereas real people have histories that can be uncovered through research, which may lead to new ways of thinking about those characters as well.

The physical possessions a character holds dear can tell readers a lot about that character. In Lesson 17, "A Lost Treasure," guest author Kristy Dempsey challenges writers to take it away by imagining that character losing a prized possession. As a writer, you'll learn a lot about this character by how he or she reacts.

If we give ourselves too much freedom as we brainstorm about a character, we may experience difficulty knowing how to start writing. Guest author Katy Duffield offers a solution in Lesson 18, "Getting Specific," by forcing some parameters on the idea-generation process. She also offers specific elements that must be included in free writing.

The lessons in this chapter can all be applied to characters in fiction as well as those in biographies and other works of nonfiction. In Lesson 19, "Characters in Nonfiction," guest author Loree Griffin Burns takes a closer look at real-world characters and how focusing on small details can provide some of the biggest insights.

In Lesson 20, "Sending Characters on the Road," guest author Anne Marie Pace invites us to plan a vacation for a character. Where would Stuart Little want to go to get away from it all? What would he pack? What if a real-life scientist or world leader needed some time away? Imagining a road trip allows us to explore another side of characters, whether they're fictional heroes, historical figures, or contemporary world leaders.

To know our characters well, we must look into their hearts, and there, we'll find not only their memories of joy but also the troubles they carry wherever they go. In Lesson 21, "What's Your Character's Knot?" we take a closer look at what's troubling a character. This view works well as a pure brainstorming strategy for fiction or as a spark for research for works of nonfiction.

No matter what you or your students are writing, it begins with the characters. When readers care about the characters at the center of the story, they'll follow those characters anywhere. Developing characters is an essential skill for writers of fiction and nonfiction alike.

JO'S MORNING WARM-UP

(Originally shared on June 11, 2012)

Today I want to talk about people—more specifically, characters and how we develop them so that they become unique, believable, lovable (or detestable, depending on your aim), and, most important, memorable.

Yesterday, I went to the memorial service of a very dear friend, Marguerite (Peg) Davol. Some of you may have used her beautiful picture books in your classrooms. My favorite is *The Paper Dragon*, illustrated by Robert Sabuda. I was asked to say a few words about Peg at the service, and it was both very difficult and very healing. Peg was a special lady. I both miss and still feel her love and light very strongly. Last night as I was trying to fall asleep, I began to think about all the things I loved about Peg: the things that made her unique, believable, lovable (always) and, memorable. Here they are in no particular order:

I remember Peg's eyes the most
how, if you dared to look in them,
you could feel them see right into your soul
how they defined her smile
and how, cliché as it is, they sparkled
they really did!
she had thin, wispy hair which she had curled once a month

and whenever she'd come from an appointment, she'd pat it gently
and grin in a pleased and mischievous kind of way
as though curly hair was also a little naughty somehow
an indulgence
she enjoyed reading the *Times* every morning
and doing the crossword
and confessing to crossing out George Bush and Dick Cheney's faces with her pencil
it feels good, she told me once, and I don't feel guilty at all!
I remember her bright blue Toyota RAV and how well she drove it
our drives to New York City, once in a snowstorm
tiny Peg at the wheel saying not to worry
and I didn't
I remember her hard-to-read handwriting
on the Christmas photo cards she sent every year
and pointing out how she was one of the few people left to still write a note
the way she said I love you with a jutted-out chin
pointed in my direction
I remember her hugs—she always squeezed with both hands
as if she were holding on to you
as if she wanted you to know she had you
it felt so good
and I try now, to hug the same way
I remember her tattered notebook with worn-soft pages
and how lovely it was to see someone at our table of writers
still using pen and paper
not hiding behind a laptop screen but
instead constantly looking up and around
listening, watching, learning,
writing it all down
how she hated the word "suddenly"

and taught us all how to avoid using it
how she referred to those she wasn't crazy about by last name
how she always showed up
even though in the final years it was very hard
she called herself a conference junkie
and made me one, too
she admitted my work was hard to take sometimes
too raw
but told me not to change it
she ate like a little bird, filling up quickly
and would always save the leftovers to bring home to her husband
she wore rings on most of her fingers
and moved her hands constantly
with a signature flick full of attitude
most often used to dismiss
but sometimes used to direct
and sometimes to emphasize a particularly good joke
I always wanted to tell her she was the grandmother I never really had
but I didn't
because I don't think she would have liked that
for me to create an age barrier between us
we were friends most importantly
colleagues
writing partners on occasion
but always friends first
and we loved each other the way friends do
and will miss each other the way friends do
she is with me, and she is not with me
but I can remember her
I can hold those memories in my heart now

and that is more than enough . . .

that is a gift.

Think of someone you love or have loved (or detested—that can be fun, too!) and make a list poem like the one above, describing all of the traits that made that person special, unique, memorable, frightening (you get the picture). Try to avoid clichés. Instead, give us specific tidbits that show how the person's eyes sparkled rather than say they did—don't fail at it like me! Once you have your list, circle your favorites. Think about why you like those traits the best. Now try to use similar ones to describe the characters in your works in progress. Give them their own particularities that might reveal something deeper about their personalities.

Jo Knowles is the author of *Read Between the Lines, Living with Jackie Chan, See You at Harry's, Pearl, Jumping Off Swings,* and *Lessons from a Dead Girl*. For more of her Morning Warm-Up prompts, visit www.joknowles.com/prompts.htm.

Lesson 13: Getting to Know Our Main Characters

By Jo Knowles

Think of this as an interview, of sorts, where you ask your characters questions to better get to know them. This applies to all ages and genres, whether you're writing a picture book, middle grade novel, young adult novel, or biography.

TODAY'S ASSIGNMENT

Interview your character(s). Remember to treat this like a freewriting exercise and have fun. Things to ask:

- What do you look like? (Remember to answer the way your character would answer.)
- Describe your bedroom. Do you have your own room? Share?
- What is your family like?
- Do you have any pets? Describe them.
- What is your favorite thing about yourself? Least favorite?
- What is your biggest pet peeve?

- What are you afraid of?
- What do you want but can't have?
- Who is your best friend?
- Who is your worst enemy?
- What do you want people to know about you but are afraid to share?

If you don't have an active work in progress, try writing this from the point of view of a character you dream up today. Maybe it will turn into a bigger idea! Or if you'd like to focus on history or science, try writing from the point of view of a favorite historical figure, scientist, or animal.

PHOTO CREDIT: ELI CARINI

Jo Knowles is the author of *Read Between the Lines, Living with Jackie Chan, See You at Harry's, Pearl, Jumping Off Swings*, and *Lessons from a Dead Girl.* Her awards and honors include *New York Times* and ALA Notable Book distinctions and the PEN New England Children's Book Discovery Award. Jo has a master's degree in children's literature from Simmons College. She has been a volunteer writing mentor at a Vermont women's prison and cotaught at a teen writing camp for several years. She teaches in the MFA program at Southern New Hampshire University. Visit her website at www.joknowles.com.

Lesson 14: In the Garden

By Jeannine Atkins

If we were all together in a room, I'd give directions for this three-part exercise by pausing for everyone to write one section before beginning the next. If you're disciplined, and like surprises, please try responding to the first prompt, then going on to the next. Because reading is usually quicker than writing, personally I'd have a hard time not skimming all the prompts, but writing always surprises me more than thinking, so the exercises should still lead you someplace new.

TODAY'S ASSIGNMENT

1. Interesting characters have problems. Creating a character on the spot or taking one from a work in progress, write down a major problem for your character.
2. Leaving that conflict behind, take your character and imagine her as being young enough to find her face near some flowers and blooms. For older characters this may be a memory of a garden where she feels free to roam around and peer close into blossoms. Write what she sees, smells, and touches. Are there particular plants, trees, or bugs that capture her attention? Describe them. She might stop to have a tea party with leaf plates and acorn cups. Does she talk to any birds or animals? Do they talk to her? Write down the dialogue. When she looks up, does she feel rain or sun? Describe the sensation. Does she find secret messages among rocks, violets, beetles, or the shade of an oak?
3. Please write what your character learned from her time in this garden. Can she use this to help solve the problem you described at the beginning of the exercise? Try writing a scene that brings the problem and the old garden together.

Jeannine Atkins writes books about history for children and teens, including *Aani and the Tree Huggers* and *Borrowed Names: Poems About Laura Ingalls Wilder, Madam C. J. Walker, Marie Curie and Their Daughters*. Her most recent book is *Views from a Window Seat: Thoughts on Writing and Life*. She teaches children's literature at the University of Massachusetts–Amherst and a graduate course in writing for children at Simmons College. Visit her website at www.Jeannineatkins.com.

Lesson 15: If Characters Ruled the Land

By Kate Messner

Even the true political junkies among us need a break from busy election seasons now and then. This prompt is inspired by The Horn Book's KidLit Election project of 2012, in which the site's editors invited readers to nominate their favorite fictional characters as Democratic or Republican candidates for the U.S. presidency. Candidates such as Charlotte A. Cavatica and The Lorax made strong showings. See www.hbook.com/2012/09/blogs/out-of-the-box/kidlit-election-2012-democratic-primary-results-are-in/.

TODAY'S ASSIGNMENT

Imagine your favorite fictional character running for president (or prime minister, or whoever's in charge where you live). Write his or her (or its?) speech to accept the nomination. Be sure to both inspire supporters and outline a clear platform of beliefs and promises. Consider what kinds of beliefs your character has and how those might shape political policy. Have fun, but be thoughtful, too.

You may also want to try this with a character from one of your own works in progress. Running for office forces you to examine what you believe and how far you're willing to go to fight for it, I suspect. Interesting stuff to ponder, wearing our characters' shoes.

Lesson 16: Studying a Character's Family

By Laura Wynkoop

I don't know about you, but I've always felt that families are kind of a mixed blessing. They love you, bug you, help you, hurt you, make you laugh, make you cry, and generally drive you crazy. But you know life wouldn't be the same without them. And you wouldn't be who you are without them.

I find it interesting to think about my favorite characters and take a good look at their families. Take Rick Riordan's hero Percy Jackson, for example. Unbeknownst to him, he's the son of Poseidon, and at the age of twelve, he's sent to a camp for demigods. If not for his father, Percy wouldn't be one of the most powerful half-bloods on the planet.

And then there's Harry Potter. After the death of his loving parents, he has to be raised by his aunt and uncle. As cruel and coldhearted as they are, their bond of blood offers Harry protection from Voldemort.

And speaking of protection, the entire plot of *The Hunger Games* hinges on Katniss's move to take Prim's place in the reaping. She would do anything, make any sacrifice, in an effort to keep her little sister safe.

These are very brief examples, of course, but I think it's helpful to evaluate how characters are affected by their family dynamics.

TODAY'S ASSIGNMENT

Take one of your characters (it can be from your work in progress or an entirely new character), and examine his or her family. Who does your character live with? Which family member is your character closest to? Why? What special bonds do they share? Who is the biggest source of tension? Why? What has happened to strain their relationship? How do specific family members influence your character's beliefs and actions? This activity works for getting to know famous people in history as well as fictional characters.

Laura Wynkoop has published poetry, articles, puzzles, lessons, and activities in numerous children's magazines, as well as educational books with Gryphon House. She also edited and contributed to *An Eyeball in My Garden—And Other Spine-Tingling Poems*, a middle grade anthology from Marshall Cavendish Children's Books. Visit her website at www.LauraWynkoop.com.

Lesson 17: A Lost Treasure

By Kristy Dempsey

At the end of this school year, the first graders were studying the elements of story through fairy tales. We talked about imagination, we talked about the cultural aspects of fairy tales from around the world, and we talked about what gave these characters believable qualities even though the stories themselves might have magical elements.

Toward the end of our unit, we watched the film *A Little Princess*. I was rather amazed as the first graders identified that Sara's locket and the importance it held for her made the story feel believable to them. One student said, "It's like her locket held everything her daddy had ever given her, and when Miss Minchin took it away from her, Sara knew she still had all that in her heart." These first graders understood the importance of emotional truth!

TODAY'S ASSIGNMENT

Think of the physical item that is most important to your main character. What does it represent? Now imagine it being lost or taken away from your main character. How would he or she respond? Sara Crewe's response, of course, was fairly noble. But what if your character pitched a fit? Or what if he or she embarked on a series of misadventures to try to recoup what was lost? (In fact, one of the funniest scenes in the movie is when Sara's friends enter Miss Minchin's office to try to get the locket back.)

Write a scene that shows the emotional importance of this physical item to your main character, and then show us how he or she responds when it is lost or taken.

Kristy Dempsey grew up in small-town South Carolina but now works as a librarian in Belo Horizonte, Brazil, a city of five million people. She is the author of *Me with You*; *Mini Racer*; *Surfer Chick*, which received starred reviews from Kirkus and *School Library Journal*; and *A Dance Like Starlight*, which received a starred review from Kirkus and is a Junior Library Guild selection. Visit her website at www.kristydempsey.com/.

Lesson 18: Getting Specific

By Katy Duffield

My favorite types of writing prompts are those that carry certain restrictions. I'll admit that I'm often too unfocused or too indecisive to write to a more general prompt such as "Write about a time when you were angry" or "Describe your childhood bedroom." These prompts are too "wide open" for me. I usually feel that the writing I'm producing with these prompts is too general (too blah!) and often not applicable to a specific story or work in progress. I seem to make more progress when I am asked to focus a little more tightly, using specifics.

A teacher in a creative writing class I recently took was a master at these types of prompts. In working through her prompts, I was amazed by the wide-ranging, atypical work I was creating. I kept asking myself, "Did I write that?" By including certain parameters within the prompts, I was led in surprising directions. I hope you'll find this type of prompt as valuable as I have.

Today's prompt will help you focus on "knowing" your character. As writers, we understand that our characters do not live in a vacuum. If we want them to resonate with readers, they have to feel real, right? One way to bring them to life is to consider what their lives were like before and what they will be like after your story takes place.

TODAY'S ASSIGNMENT

Take the character you're working with (or one you think you would like to write about), and write about a time when that character is five to ten years older than he or she is within your story. Then go back and write about a time where he or she is five to ten years younger. You can adjust the time range, of course, to suit the current age of your main character. Nonfiction note: This exercise works well for historical figures as well as for fictional characters.

To follow the more specific prompt type that I mentioned above, try this: within your writings, include an argument, a food that no one wants to eat, two specific place-names, and an article of sports clothing.

Ready. Set. Get specific!

PHOTO CREDIT: TIA WIND PHOTOGRAPHY

Award-winning author Katy Duffield writes both fiction and nonfiction for children and young adults and is the author of more than twenty books, including *Farmer McPeepers and His Missing Milk Cows*, *California History for Kids: Missions, Miners, and Moviemakers in the Golden State*, and two forthcoming picture books, *Aliens Get the Sniffles, Too* and *Loud Lula.* Katy has also written for many children's magazines and educational publishers. Visit her website at www.katyduffield.com.

Lesson 19: Characters in Nonfiction

By Loree Griffin Burns

Be honest: Are you surprised that a writer like me—one who writes about ocean trash and honey bees and backyard science—would choose to write a feature on the topic of characterization? Do you think of character development as a strictly fictional device? For a long time, I did, too. For most of my reading and writing life, in fact, I had it in my head that fiction writers were storytellers, and nonfiction writers were, well, reporters. The former, in my misguided mind, had access to all the neat storytelling tools—characterization, setting, conflict, foreshadowing, pacing, and so on—and the latter were meant to simply share the facts.

This misunderstanding was blown to bits when I read *The Beak of the Finch* back in 1995. In this nonfiction title, Jonathan Weiner opened my eyes to an important truth: All writers must use every tool at their disposal to make their storytelling engaging. Weiner shared the true story of Peter and Rosemary Grant—evolutionary biologists who have recorded, over the course of more than twenty years of Galápagos fieldwork, the process of evolution in action—in a book that reads like a novel. (For the record, it remains one of my all-time favorites in the genre.)

Let readers know your character, ground those readers in a setting, entice them with a unique voice, thrill them with tension and strong pacing, include telling details and rich dialogue, and don't forget to share memorable images, both literal and figurative. Structure your story so that all these elements work together, pulling your readers through the narrative, page by page. These are tasks for all of us who share stories, whether the stories we tell are true or are born from our imaginations.

Here's an example from my own writing life. I'm drafting a book about an entomologist. Clint McFarland is a passionate scientist and a true lover of insects, and yet his job (and this is the heart of my story) is to kill every last Asian long-horned beetle in North America. A man who kills beetles for a living will be hard enough for my young readers to take. When I tell them that the way one kills this particular beetle is by cutting down and chipping every single host tree in its range—no matter if those trees shade a schoolyard or sport backyard tree houses—well, I might lose those readers. Before I share this part of the story, then, it's important that I let readers see Clint as the caring and passionate guy he is. This man adores insects. Passionately. Deeply. How do I show this side of Clint? By sharing his personality on the page. By paying close attention to how I introduce him. In short, with careful characterization.

To this end, I spent several hours last week reading through all the interviews I've conducted with Clint. (Our five in-person interviews have resulted in forty-one pages of transcribed notes.) I hunted for details that will help readers understand the type of guy Clint is. There was the surprising confession that he cuts his long hair every so often to donate a ponytail to Locks of Love. I told you he was a nice guy! Evidence of his passion for insects was everywhere: the set of ladybug life cycle toys on his office bookshelves ("biologically accurate egg, larva, pupa, and adult," he told me), the worn copy of Thomas Eisner's *For Love of Insects*.

My favorite detail by far, though, was a scene I recorded when a member of Clint's staff found an insect in the parking lot and brought it in to show Clint during our interview. "You'll love this," the staff member said, holding out a cup with a dead Dobsonfly inside. I'd never seen one before, but I can now tell you this: Dobsonflies are sort of hideous. This particular beast was more than two inches long, but gained almost another full inch from the set of curved, scythe-like mandibles stretching out the top of its head. The mandibles looked like pincers, and as I was trying to figure out if they could pierce human skin, Clint turned the creature into his bare hand, marveled over its "amazing wings," and ran a gentle finger over its "gorgeous mandibles."

If I can craft a chapter that shares these details with readers, I won't need to tell them Clint is a compassionate man with a heart for insects. They will have learned it for themselves.

TODAY'S ASSIGNMENT

The good thing about this prompt, I think, is that everyone can play along, fiction and nonfiction writers alike. Choose a character from one of your works in progress—a real person (if you are working on a nonfiction piece) or a made-up person (if you are working on a novel or a short story). Comb through all your files, physical or mental, on this person, and pull out the details that tell you the most about his or her character.

If this process feels overwhelming, start small. Does he or she have an office? Go there and look around. Is it messy? Or crazy-neat? What does the desktop look like? Is there a half glass of orange juice on board? A reusable thermal coffee mug? An army of old Dunkin' Donuts cups? What is the dust situation? Is there anything hanging on the walls? Are there bookshelves? Are the books on them just what you'd expect to see, or does something there surprise you?

I think you get the idea. All writers can benefit from some quality time spent observing the little details—settings, habits, dialogue, and actions—that tell us who our characters are. Nonfiction writers will finish this exercise realizing, if they hadn't already, that the best way to get these details is to meet your subject—or someone with a passion for your topic—in person. Push your nerves aside and set up that interview!

Loree Griffin Burns writes award-winning Scientists in the Field titles such as *Beetle Busters*, *Tracking Trash*, and *The Hive Detectives*. She is also the author of *Citizen Scientists: Be Part of a Scientific Discovery in Your Own Backyard* and *Handle with Care: An Unusual Butterfly Journey*. Visit her website at www.loreeburns.com.

Lesson 20: Sending Characters on the Road

By Anne Marie Pace

You'll have to forgive me if I seem dreamy; as I write this, I'm physically at home, jotting notes between driving kids to activities and doing laundry, but my head and heart are still walking along the shore of Folly Beach, South Carolina, searching for a perfect shell. For a variety of reasons, that was our first family vacation in four years. My vacation week has inspired this quick-write exercise for you.

TODAY'S ASSIGNMENT

Choose a character, either one from your work in progress or a character you create just for this exercise. Don't feel as if you need to answer these questions one at a time. Read them through with this character in mind, and then write something in response: a letter, a poem, a journal entry, a descriptive paragraph—whatever flows.

First: Has this character ever gone on a vacation? If your character is from the type of family that takes yearly trips, which one has been the favorite? Why? Does she go to the same place every year? Who is there? What does she like to do there? Is it boring or comforting to go to the same place? How does she feel if that trip changes? Or is it a different trip every year? If so, how does she feel about changing it up all the time? Does she like exploring new places or does she regret being unable to return?

At the other end of the spectrum, perhaps your character has never been on vacation. Why has she been unable to vacation? Is it a financial issue or is there another reason? How far has she been from home? Are there any events she looks forward to during summer? Does she have friends who are able to vacation with their families? Is she jealous? Is she happy for them? Would she be scared to leave home? Does she have a dream place to vacation? Is there something she could do to make a vacation possible (win a contest, win the lottery, convince a neighbor or friend to do something that relieves parental stress)?

These questions are somewhat slanted toward contemporary fiction. If you are writing in another genre, feel free to replace "vacation" (in our contemporary sense) with "travel." If the setting of your story is a world you have built, how does that world deal with a desire to travel and/or rest? How does your character feel about those societal customs or expectations?

Think about what you have discovered about your character. What part of that person is illuminated? Is there a parallel between your character's experiences on vacation and what he or she is facing today? How might this revelation develop or connect to your plans for your work?

Anne Marie Pace is the author of *Vampirina Ballerina* and its sequel, *Vampirina Ballerina Hosts a Sleepover*, both illustrated by LeUyen Pham and published by Disney-Hyperion. She has also written *A Teacher for Bear* and *Never Ever Talk to Strangers* for Scholastic Book Clubs. Visit her website at www.annemariepace.com.

Lesson 21: What's Your Character's Knot?

By Kate Messner

I'm working through a novel revision right now with a huge focus on character. Specifically, I'm studying the growth of my main character throughout the book, because if a character doesn't grow and change . . . well, there's not much of a story to be told.

I've been reading *Plot Versus Character: A Balanced Approach to Writing Great Fiction* by Jeff Gerke. This book takes a hard look at what we really need to make our characters live on the page. Every character, Gerke says, should start with a problem, which he calls the character's "knot."

> *Whether he knows about it or is working to correct it or not, the knot is messing up his life. (Gerke 2010, 85)*

TODAY'S ASSIGNMENT

What is your character's knot? We're talking about a character's internal problem, rather than the bear that may be about to eat him. I'm not denying that facing death by bear maul is a problem, but it's not the internal struggle targeted in this exercise. If you have a work in progress, write a little about your main character's knot (or your antagonist's knot; bad guys have knots, too, you know!).

This process works well with both heroes and villains from history as well as fictional characters. It can also be a great literary analysis tool when you write as a reader. Try writing about the knot of the main character in one of your favorite books.

Q+A - THE BEST OF Q-AND-A WEDNESDAY: WHERE TO START—CHARACTERS OR PLOT?

What comes first, the chicken or the egg? Substitute *character* and *plot* for *chicken* and *egg*, and you have a classic question for writers. Here's how some authors answered it during our summer Teachers Write camp.

QUESTION: I've been reading Stephen King's book on writing, and he pushes the idea of not focusing so much on plot when starting out with a story. Instead, he suggests beginning with situations, letting characters unfold in those situations, and letting the story unfold from there. Do you start with a plot plan when you write? Or does it develop gradually?

ANSWERS:

I've written books the way King describes, but I find that after wandering/getting to know the character and watching him or her respond to the situation for a while, I reach a point where I step back and say, "Okay . . . now where are we going with this?" And then I outline. I think it also depends on what kind of book you're writing. If a story is more character driven, I think this makes a lot of sense, but for something like a mystery or fast-paced thriller, it may be better to start with at least a rough plot outline, even if it changes a lot along the way.

~Kate Messner, author of *All the Answers, How to Read a Story,* and the Ranger in Time series

The funny thing about that advice is that Stephen King's early stories were very strongly plotted. He is a brilliant enough writer that the situations he thinks up lead to compelling stories. Two examples: A man pays a service to help him stop smoking, and then learns they work like thugs, using strong-arm techniques. A man is forced to walk on a penthouse ledge after he is caught having an affair with a rich man's wife. In each case, the crucial thing to notice is that it starts out with someone wanting something (to stop smoking/to be with the one you love) and ends up with a greater desire (to avoid being hurt/to avoid death).

As for your question about how others start out, I often start with a concept phrased in the form of a "what if" question. Even if the spark came in another fashion, such as observation or a stray thought, it usually ends up phrased as "What if . . . ?" But many writers start with a character, or other aspect. I will, on occasion, just start writing, or write an opening hook, then keep going to see what happens.

~David Lubar, author of *Hidden Talents* and the Weenies short story collections

I think there's no escaping an outline at some point in the process, and if you're writing a highly structured kind of story such as a mystery, you'll be well served to outline sooner. I think if you have a series that is written on a tight deadline, an outline early in the process is a good idea as well.

The danger of outlining too early is that you miss the spontaneous and fresh response to a situation that a character might make that really makes her ring true and opens up possibilities in the plot you hadn't considered before. Part of the excitement for a writer comes when a character makes an unanticipated choice. It can add depth to a story and keep what is often a long and arduous process interesting.

Ultimately, I think each author finds her method. I tend to wait until after a first draft to outline, but I'm a slower writer working in a more character-driven vein with single titles. If I were to write a series, I'd probably approach things differently.

~Rosanne Parry, author of *Written in Stone* and *Heart of a Shepherd*

Q+A - THE BEST OF Q-AND-A WEDNESDAY: CONNECTING WITH CHARACTERS

As readers, we all know the feeling of making strong connections with characters in a book. If we care about the characters and connect with them, we'll follow them anywhere the story goes.

QUESTION: Do you have advice for really connecting with the characters that you are writing? Do you do anything special, some kind of writing prompt maybe that gets you into the head of those characters?

ANSWERS:

I take a variety of approaches when "building characters." Lately, I've taken to creating character profiles. With each character, I list what they look like, what they wear, and who they live with (building those characters as well, even if they don't appear in the book), and name their favorites–food, music, books, websites, hobbies, subjects, and so on.

To create voice, I always need to say the character's lines out loud. It also helps me make sure I don't confuse character voices.

~Phil Bildner, author of *The Soccer Fence*

When I really need to get into a character, I have the other characters each write a short essay about her.

~David Lubar, author of *Hidden Talents* and the Weenies short story collections

Getting inside the head of a character is one of those things that happens to me as I write the story, so it's not something I prep for. Usually, my characters have one characteristic that stands out to me most at the beginning, and I sort of build them around that. Often, I have to go back and layer in more details as I get to know her–it's a very messy process and probably not the most organized or efficient, but it's what (sort of) works for me.

~Joanne Levy, author of *Small Medium at Large*

When I am working on a book, whether nonfiction or fiction, I love to surround myself with things that help me keep my characters/my subject in my head.

As far as a writing prompt that helps get into characters' heads, I like to imagine the places my characters sleep. I think not only about what might be in their rooms, but also about what they might see out their windows.

~Nancy Castaldo, author of *Sniffer Dogs: How Dogs (and Their Noses) Save the World*

Q+A - THE BEST OF Q-AND-A WEDNESDAY: CHARACTERS AND DIALOGUE—WHEN TO CUT

Sometimes, when writers revise, it means adding description and details. Sometimes, though, it's paring down that leads to improvement. That might mean trimming bits of dialogue or description, or it might mean eliminating a character entirely.

QUESTION: What are some things that help you decide if a character needs to be cut from a book?

ANSWERS:

If a character performs a single function, I always look to see if that function can be done by someone else (or eliminated). If all scenes with a certain character fail to advance the plot, I kill that darling. If a character strikes me as uninteresting, he's history.

~David Lubar, author of *Hidden Talents* and the Weenies short story collections

Usually, if I'm having questions about a character on a second or third revision pass, I'll make a list of what that character's roles are in the book (for example, sidekick, contrasts with main character, tells a secret, and so on) and then decide if another character that already exists can take over those jobs.

–Kate Messner, author of *All the Answers, How to Read a Story,* and the Ranger in Time series

I look at overall numbers of characters in the book and ask myself how many people I'm asking my reader to care about. Usually keeping the focus on three or four key characters works best. There are many books with sibling groups of four, for example. It's harder to write effectively about a larger group.

If you're on the fence about a character, try writing the story without her and see what happens. Save your previous draft and you're not risking much. You can always go back to an earlier version.

–Rosanne Parry, author of *Written in Stone* and *Heart of a Shepherd*

With the young adult novel I'm currently revising, I loved all my characters and could visualize them all, but multiple readers told me there were too many and they got confused. I didn't like this idea at first, believe me. You really have to learn to trust your gut as far as feedback goes. I reread some of the first chapters of my favorite current books and counted characters. In the end, because I kept getting the same feedback, I decided to honor this and give it a try. Turns out they were right.

–Erin Dealey, author of *Deck the Walls*

QUESTION: My question is about dialogue. I love to write it, but sometimes I find my characters spending too much time chatting. What are your tips to keep a story moving while not losing important exchanges between characters?

ANSWERS:

In a first draft, I think it's important to just let your characters talk. See where the conversation goes. You might find yourself and your story in a new and interesting place! When you get to the revision stage, read the scene out loud to yourself. The unnecessary or ramble-y parts will jump out at you. Also, this is a place where having trusted first readers or a critique group can really help.

–Dayna Lorentz, author of *No Safety in Numbers*

I have that issue as well sometimes. Depending on the situation your characters are in, you can intersperse short actions into the dialogue that might reflect how they're feeling, without you (or they) explicitly telling us. A character who is worried or distracted might spoon seven teaspoons of sugar into her coffee cup. Someone confused or frightened might have to try three times before she gets her key into the lock. A flush might creep across someone's cheeks. An angry person might set his coffee mug down so hard, the rest of the dishes jump. Often I write the dialogue and then go back in to see if it can be broken up with action (or substituted for action if there's too much of it).

~Sarah Albee, author of *Poop Happened: A History of the World from the Bottom Up* and *Bugged: How Insects Changed History*

I once read a writing handbook that said dialogue should be used as sparingly as spice; the book included samples and challenged the reader to examine how much dialogue appears on a single page of any book. I was shocked to see some of my favorite books sometimes had only one or two lines on a good number of pages.

That said, I think it's perfectly fine to have runs of dialogue as long as the narrative contains a balance of interior dialogue. My books have plenty of dialogue, but as dialogue raises issues between characters, I might have my main character alone as she finishes the bike ride home, reviewing what was said or showing how she felt about what was said by how she rides her bike: she hammers on the pedals, or maybe she skids, leaving a solid black mark on the sidewalk–especially if the sidewalk is in front of a house that is home to someone related to the problem.

Hailee Richardson's bike does a lot of the "talking" in A Whole Lot of Lucky.

~Danette Haworth, author of *A Whole Lot of Lucky* and *Violet Raines Almost Got Struck by Lightning*

CHAPTER 5
Point of View, Voice, and Mood

Voice is one of the hardest elements of good writing to teach; most readers will simply tell you that they know a great voice when they "hear" it. But there are strategies that writers of all ages can use to develop voice, whether the work in progress is poetry, fiction, or nonfiction. Voice, point of view, and mood are all close cousins in the world of writing, and in this chapter, we'll explore some writing prompts and lessons for all three.

In Lesson 22, "Through a Dog's Eyes," guest author Dayna Lorentz invites us to take on an unusual point of view, writing—and seeing the world—through the eyes of a canine friend. This is an excellent prompt for developing voice in fiction and an equally great exercise to use in the classroom when students are exploring topics in the content areas. Just change "Through a Dog's Eyes" to "A Paramecium's Point of View" or "Through

Thomas Jefferson's Eyes," and you have a lesson that extends to writing in virtually any subject.

"When Is a Popsicle More Than a Popsicle?" In Lesson 23, Linda Urban takes a look at the objects in our characters' lives and the ways in which different characters might view those objects differently. Both of these first two lessons challenge us as writers to view the world–and the specific objects in it–through a unique lens.

In Lesson 24, "Listening for Voice," guest author Erin Dealey uses stream-of-consciousness writing as a vehicle to explore voice through objects and the stories left behind by the people who have touched them.

In Lesson 25, "Setting a Mood," author Jenny Meyerhoff invites us to create a mood by looking at the same room in various ways, through the eyes of people experiencing different emotional states.

People are always talking about the weather in real life, but sometimes it's easy to forget about this element of setting in writing. In Lesson 26, "Add Rain," guest author Megan Miranda invites writers to let it rain and then watch how the weather changes the mood of the scene and how the characters respond. This is a fun prompt to explore with classes studying historical events. For example, how might rain have changed the Boston Tea Party or the Battle of Gettysburg?

Playing around with different settings, emotions, and points of view gives writers practice adjusting the voice and mood for any kind of text. In works of nonfiction, the voice might be more formal, depending on the purpose. Writers of all ages must have a well-stocked toolbox of strategies for developing voice so that each piece of writing can connect with its intended audience.

JO'S MORNING WARM-UP

I spent last week on vacation with my family in Maine. One night, I went to dinner at the Flatbread Company in Portland. Outside, they have "Before I die . . ." chalkboards for people to write their hopes on.

Some were silly. Some were poignant. Some were unsurprising. And some were beautifully unselfish. Before I die, I want to . . .

. . . finish this run!

. . . go to Israel.

. . . love everyone unconditionally.

. . . act in a play.

. . . see a polar bear.

. . . have my moment of Zen.

And some were very familiar. Before I die, I want to. . .

. . . write a book.

Your warm-up today is to complete this statement yourself, and then do the same for each of your main characters, whether you are writing fiction, nonfiction, a novel, or a picture book. Think carefully about how each character might respond. Would he or she write the answer in public? Answer in his or her head? Or would the person be too afraid to answer? Write the scene for each one, carefully describing the person's reaction to seeing the statement, and then the thought process for filling it in.

Jo Knowles is the author of *Read Between the Lines, Living with Jackie Chan, See You at Harry's, Pearl, Jumping Off Swings,* and *Lessons from a Dead Girl.* For more of her Morning Warm-Up prompts, visit www.joknowles.com/prompts.htm.

Lesson 22: Through a Dog's Eyes

By Dayna Lorentz

My first book series, Dogs of the Drowned City (Scholastic 2012), is an animal fantasy adventure for middle grade readers, and is told from the point of view of Shep, a German shepherd. The biggest challenge in writing this series was trying to capture how Shep, as opposed to a human (a.k.a. me), perceives the world. I wanted to create for readers the world of the story as Shep and my other dog characters experienced it. To do this, I focused on three things.

First, I tried to describe everything using a dog's primary senses: smell and sound, then sight. This is really hard for a sight-dependent human like me. It means talking about what the grass smells like and how it whispers as it moves in the wind, before talking about the fact that it's green.

Second, I had to think about the human world from a dog's point of view. This meant figuring out what would most interest a dog in the human world. I guessed smelly things like socks and leftovers. I also had to think about how dogs might describe things that are totally alien to them, such as vacuum cleaners. (During school visits, I ask kids to come up with their own descriptions for a vacuum cleaner. Shep calls them "floor suckers.")

Finally, I changed the language I used in the book to reflect how I thought a dog would talk. I made up dog idioms and sayings and tried to put a doggy spin on my descriptions, such as describing daybreak as "the tails of dawn wagging in the sky."

These steps forced me to get out of my own, limited point of view and put myself into the perspective of another person/dog, an exercise that can be helpful even if you're not writing from the viewpoint of a different species. I found that I had to do similar, though perhaps not as extreme, exercises when writing my YA trilogy, No Safety in Numbers (Dial 2012–2014): How would this particular character describe the smell of the food court at the mall? What things would she notice that maybe I wouldn't?

TODAY'S ASSIGNMENT

The first Dogs of the Drowned City book, *The Storm*, is about a pack of pets trying to survive a superstorm that wipes out Miami. A lot of my research, therefore, focused on Hurricane Katrina and the thousands of pets left stranded in the city when people were evacuated and told they could not bring their furry family members with them. Some of the pets were stranded, finding safety on top of cars in the midst of the flood.

Write a scene from the point of view of a dog stranded in Hurricane Katrina. Focus on making the scene as doggy as possible. Try employing these tricks:

- Describe how things smell first, then by sight.
- Although a dog's eyesight is better than a human's, a dog sees in a limited palate of colors, mostly yellow or blue. These dogs would not, for example, talk about the bright red sedan submerged across the street from them.
- As a dog, you have four paws—use them!
- Dogs can communicate in many different ways. They bark and growl, but they also use their ears, tails, and stance to signal how they're feeling.

If you're deeply submerged in your work in progress and don't want to surface, try taking a scene, maybe the scene you're working on, and list all the ways in which you would describe and talk about your surroundings. Then make a separate list for how your character would describe and talk about those same things. How are they the same? Should they be the same, or have you missed an opportunity to move the story further from yourself and into the space of your character? Think about the metaphors you're using: are they yours, or do they reflect the character's point of view?

One of my characters in No Safety is *very* different from me. When I was writing from his perspective, I wrote his chapters, and then went back and edited all the sentences to make them less complex. I took out all the metaphorical language because it didn't ring true; it was me talking about him and his situation, but not really *being* him in that situation.

Dayna Lorentz is the author of the Dogs of the Drowned City series (Scholastic) and the No Safety in Numbers trilogy (Dial/Kathy Dawson Books). She holds an MFA in creative writing and literature from Bennington College. A former attorney, Dayna is now a full-time writer and lives with her husband, two kids, and dogs in Vermont. Visit her website at www.daynalorentz.com.

Lesson 23: When Is a Popsicle More Than a Popsicle?

By Linda Urban

I like certain objects to have a different meaning for different characters in a book. Sometimes I start a web with that object in the center—Popsicles, for example (see Figure 5.1)—and then connect from there to the places that Popsicles occur in the story, the people who eat them or talk about or buy them, and then all the different associations that those people and places have with the Popsicles. Sometimes what I find surprises me and gives me details that I can use as I revise. For one character, I might find that sharing a Popsicle turns out to be a supreme symbol of friendship. For another, it's just a sticky mess on her fingers.

Note: This activity and photo originally appeared in *Real Revision*, courtesy of Linda Urban.

FIGURE 5.1
Popsicle web

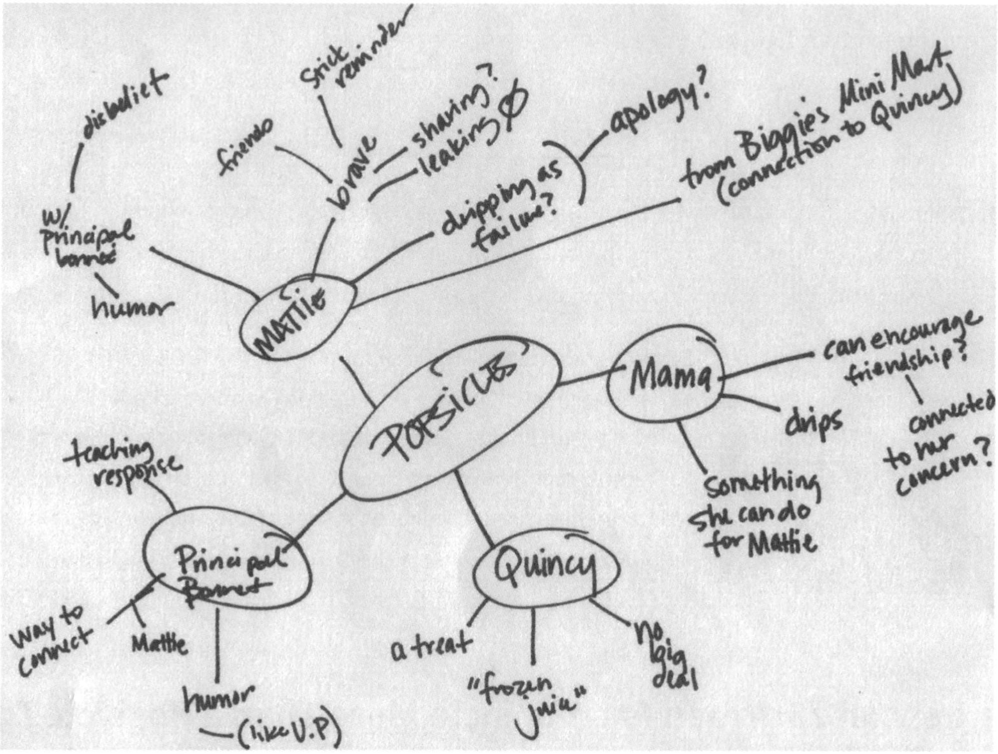

TODAY'S ASSIGNMENT

Think of an object from your work in progress. If you don't have a work in progress, try this with a book that you love as a reader. Choose an object that might mean different things to different characters in the story, and put it in the middle of an idea web. Then brainstorm all the places that object appears in the story (or all the places it might be added) and what it could mean in different settings, to different characters.

Linda Urban is the author of three novels for young readers: *A Crooked Kind of Perfect, Hound Dog True*, and *The Center of Everything*, which the *New York Times* called homey, funny, and "Thornton Wilderish." Her picture books are *Little Red Henry* and *Mouse Was Mad*, which was a Children's Choice Award finalist. Before turning her attention to writing, she spent ten years as marketing director for Vroman's Bookstore. Visit her website at www.lindaurbanbooks.com.

Lesson 24: Listening for Voice

By Erin Dealey

When I participated in my first Writer's Project summer seminar, I remember making sure my writing was grammatically correct. After all, I taught English, right? The result was a textbook tone that had me zoning out by the end of the opening paragraph, a stark contrast to the plays and skits I'd written for my drama students.

Which brings us to voice. I've heard many editors say that voice is what hooks the reader. Nonfiction needs an engaging voice, too. Some editors say you can teach form and plot, but you can't teach voice. I disagree. The breakthrough for me came when I realized that a big part of teaching theater is voice. Voice comes from learning who you are, and not being afraid to share that honesty with others.

If your students are like mine, sharing voice takes tremendous courage. It emerges first in journals and quick-writes, and I always make a point to comment when a student's voice shows up on the page. Like this acrostic I got from Darin A., one of my seniors who bristled at any assignment from an authority figure . . .

Darin

Ain't

Really

Into

No

Acrostics.

The day I used Darin's writing as an excellent example of voice, his writing took off. Voice freed him to see writing and words as power, not just as a means by which to complete his assignment.

Voice and vocabulary, sentence structure and pace (long sentences or short, choppy ones and/or fragments) grow from your character—or the character of your narrator.

One way to release student voices is by warming up with a stream-of-consciousness format I call Clearing the Cobwebs. (The following is what I tell my students. Try it!)

CLEARING THE COBWEBS

When I say "Go,"
write three words
per line (stream
of consciousness—not
laundry or grocery list . . .)
until you are
told to stop
(usually three to five minutes).
If your mind
is blank, start
with I don't
know what to
write, or a
line from your
favorite song. If
you get stuck
on a word,
DON'T STOP WRITING.
Write your last
word word word
over and over
until something clicks.
Don't think—WRITE!

The cool thing about this cobweb prewriting exercise is that students think it's so ridiculous, they let go of *trying to write*, and their authentic voices emerge.

Another way to approach voice is to refer to it as eavesdropping. Creating the voice of a character is easier if you think of it like acting in the theater: being someone else for a while. Stop thinking, and listen.

The voice of my picture book *Deck the Walls* came easily because I originally wrote it for my high school theater students to perform at a holiday assembly, and I could hear their voices.

TODAY'S ASSIGNMENT

For this prompt, you'll need to select an object. Anything will do: an antique, a child's toy, a family memento, and so on. Each object, like a seashell that whispers of the ocean's roar, has a unique story to tell. All you have to do is eavesdrop and write it down.

The stories have been left on the object by all who have come in contact with it: the person who made it; the one who sold it; the one who purchased it, traded for it, or received it as a gift; the person who tossed it in the attic; and the one who found it again. All of these people have left their stories for you to find.

No two individuals will hear the same story, because the object knows which one you want to hear.

Don't think! (Students love this rule.) *Listen!* (And write down what you hear.)

Erin Dealey writes board books and picture books, including *Deck the Walls* (Sleeping Bear Press 2013), as well as middle grade and YA novels and raps. She's also an English/theater teacher and Area 3 Writing Project presenter (University of California at Davis), and heads the theater department at Sugarloaf Fine Arts Camp each summer. Visit her website at www.erindealey.com.

Lesson 25: Setting a Mood

By Jenny Meyerhoff

When I am writing a short story, a picture book, or a novel, one of my main goals is to make the reader feel something. This may be my most important goal, but often I get caught up in the plotting, the clever wordplay, or the characterization, and I forget about the mood. When the writer isn't deliberate about mood, the reader is often left emotionally cold.

I define mood as the overall emotional resonance of a piece of writing. Although a novel as a whole has a mood, each scene also has its own mood that relates to the overall mood. For example, if the overall mood of a novel is sad, then the moods of scenes may vary from heartbreaking to bittersweet but will likely not extend as far as giddy excitement, unless there is a great reason for that emotion.

Often when I'm writing a first draft, I forget to think about mood, and while this is okay, at some point I need to go back and check that what I've written isn't at odds with the mood I meant to create. Maybe I wrote about the desolation of gray snow and bare trees in the same scene that my character got up the nerve to ask for what she wanted and got it. My reader is going to have a hard time knowing what to feel. When I revise, I pick details that echo what my character is feeling and describe them in ways that evoke a certain feeling.

TODAY'S ASSIGNMENT

Get a blank piece of paper, and in a few sentences, write a bare-bones factual description of the room that you are in right now. For example: one brown desk, a wooden bookshelf, a rectangular window. Use all five senses if you can. How does the room smell and feel, and what sounds do you hear? Get up and walk around. Pick things up. Touch them.

Now imagine that you are creating a scene in that room with a character who is feeling terrified. What would that character notice about the room? How would it be different from the emotionless, factual description? Perhaps the way the clock ticks? The way the door sticks? The fact that the door doesn't lock? Write a paragraph describing the room from this character's point of view. Don't tell us that he or she is terrified, but make it clear from the description.

Now write from the point of view of a character who is in love.

Now write from the point of view of a character who is impatient, sad, or angry.

Extension: If you have a work in progress, pick a scene, and write the emotion you want your reader to feel at the top of the page. Now read through and notice all the details you've included that evoke that emotion, all the places you could add detail that would add layers of emotion, all the places you've created an emotional response at odds with the mood you intended.

Jenny Meyerhoff is the author of a young adult novel, *Queen of Secrets*, and three books for young readers: *Sami's Sleepaway Summer*, *Third Grade Baby*, and *The Barftastic Life of Louie Burger*, a story about an aspiring stand-up comic with an unusual catchphrase. Jenny lives in Riverwoods, Illinois, with her family. Visit her website at www.jennymeyerhoff.com.

Lesson 26: Add Rain

By Megan Miranda

I have a confession: I am not an outliner. Because of this, my first drafts are very much discovery drafts. This is an exercise I do whenever I get stuck with the external plot (and as someone who typically has to write nearly an entire draft before finding the right plot, this happens a lot):

Add rain.

Rain makes things happen: Things go wrong in the rain. Accidents happen. Houses flood. People are late, appointments are missed, and plans are canceled. Evidence gets washed away. Strangers help each other on the side of the road, people share umbrellas, and people meet. Or people don't meet.

Rain reveals character: Do your characters carry umbrellas, or are they totally unprepared? Do they stomp in the puddles? Does she run with a newspaper over her head? Or smile because she gets to wear those totally impractical neon-green galoshes she spent way too much money on?

Something as simple as changing the weather opens me up to many other possibilities. It's my way of brainstorming inside a scene. Truth is, the rain doesn't always make the cut during revision, but the heart of the scene does. The events, the character reactions—they become my story.

TODAY'S ASSIGNMENT

In whatever scene you're currently writing (or if you're starting something new), try this: make it rain. If it's already raining, make it snow. See what happens. See how your character reacts.

It's always a surprise for me.

(Right now, I'm about halfway through a first draft. I'm pretty sure it's been raining for a month straight.)

If you don't have a fictional work in progress, try this quick-write with a favorite scene from any favorite novel. Play weather god and change one of the scenes by making it rain. What happens?

Megan Miranda is the author of *Fracture* and *Hysteria*. She was a scientist and high school teacher before writing *Fracture*, which came out of her fascination with scientific mysteries—especially those associated with the brain. Megan has a bachelor's degree in biology from the Massachusetts Institute of Technology and spent her post-college years either rocking a lab coat or reading books. She lives near Charlotte, North Carolina, where she volunteers as an MIT educational counselor. Visit her website at www.meganmiranda.com/.

Q+A - THE BEST OF Q-AND-A WEDNESDAY: POINT OF VIEW

Voice is one of the most sought-after elements in writing, but what is it, exactly? How do we work on building our voices as writers at the same time we choose points of view for our stories and let our characters' voices shine as well?

QUESTION: I had originally started my writing piece in the first person, but switched it to the third person. It seems to flow much better. How do authors determine which approach to take to their novels? Is one way generally used more than others?

ANSWERS:

First person is much more common, because it is more natural. We all talk and tell stories. Writing in first person is a lot like talking. If I remember correctly, there was a time, decades ago, when third person was nearly mandatory for children's books. As for which to choose, I generally use first person unless there are a lot of things the reader needs to know that the main character can't possibly know. (Interesting side note: many recent huge books, including the Harry Potter *series, are written in third person.) I think you gave a good tip when you mentioned that you tried a switch and it worked. Perhaps, for some people, it would be worthwhile to experiment with both viewpoints early on.*

~David Lubar, author of *Hidden Talents* and the Weenies short story collections

Ursula Le Guin wrote a great short book, Steering the Craft, *that I use all the time. She's got a chapter in which she writes the same scene over and over, using every possible point of view, including first, third, omniscient, and narrated by a secondary character. It's very interesting, and I've found it useful in my own writing. On my Goodreads page, I keep track of point of view in the stories I've read, which helps when I'm looking for familiar examples.*

~Rosanne Parry, author of *Written in Stone* and *Heart of a Shepherd*

My natural voice is first present, so I almost always write in it. But I wrote one of my manuscripts in first past because I wanted the "looking back" feeling of past. It was amazing how hard it was to veer away from my natural voice. I'm still not sure which that manuscript should be. But I do think the pull of our natural voice–even if that's third person, which it is for some–is also something to consider.

~Gae Polisner, author of *The Pull of Gravity* and *The Summer of Letting Go*

Usually, when I begin writing a book, a certain point of view rises to the top of my head and that's where I begin. If it works, I stick with it, but if I have the sense that the story or voice feels forced, I'll often stop and try rewriting from a different point of view. Do note that although first person may seem to be more common, a close, limited third person still gives that personal viewpoint but also gives you a little more freedom as far as the language you use and the descriptions you offer.

~Kate Messner, author of *All the Answers, How to Read a Story,* and the Ranger in Time series

My book Sleeping Beauty's Daughters *started out with two narrators speaking in the first person, morphed into one first-person point of view, and now is told through the other main character's point of view. And I'm in the middle of a work in progress that has one version in third person, one version in first. I still don't know which I'm going to go with. First person has the benefit of allowing you as the writer to be in your character's head and see through her eyes. But that can also be limiting, as you can see* only *through her eyes. First person can also create a more immediate connection between the character and readers. But third has its own benefits, giving you as the writer far more omniscience–the ability to see and describe more than the main character can see. Which point of view you use depends entirely on the work and your own purpose–and it might not be clear as you begin writing. My own experience proves that it isn't necessarily set in stone until the book is published!*

~Diane Zahler, author of *Sleeping Beauty's Daughters* and *The Black Death*

Sometimes choosing the right point of view is a matter of experimenting. For Want to Go Private? *I originally thought it would have to be written in third person, because the main character would be missing for a good third of the book. I wrote twelve thousand words and something was wrong. It wasn't working. I loved the story, but I hated how I was telling it. It seemed flat.*

Then I had this idea for a different structure for the book where it could be told in first per-

son, but with a twist in the point of view. I talked to my editor about it and she agreed, and so I started over, and suddenly the manuscript came alive. So play around. You might not want to be as slow to figure out you're on the wrong track as I was, but writing a chapter in each point of view could help you figure it out.

~Sarah Darer Littman, author of *Want to Go Private?* and *Backlash*

QUESTION: I am currently working on a YA novel, and I am struggling with point of view. Sometimes I find myself writing in first person, but then I catch myself switching to third. Is it okay to switch throughout?

ANSWERS:

Deciding on point of view can be tricky. Sometimes a voice comes to you fully formed and strong. *Other times, it can be wishy-washy. But you will have to choose one or the other for sure. For both* Pearl *and* Lessons from a Dead Girl, *I wrote the entire first drafts in third person before I realized that choice was limiting me. So I switched to first to see if that would help. I also switched tense from past to present tense. That combination changed everything!*

~Jo Knowles, author of *Read Between the Lines, Living with Jackie Chan* and *See You at Harry's*

Point of view is one of those decisions you need to make about your work, along with setting, time period, and so on.

I've written my novels in first person so I can be completely in the heads of my main characters. It brings immediacy, but also limitations because the reader can't know any more than the main character knows. Other writers prefer third person, so the reader is given more than one perspective.

Think of your point of view as a video camera. If you choose first person, only your main character holds the camera. Everything is from his or her view, or realm of experience.

If you choose third person, limited, the camera has more room to roam, but is mainly from the viewpoint of one character.

If you choose third person, omniscient, your camera can go inside the head of any character and to any location, regardless of what's happening with your main character.

Think about which one would best serve your story and stick with it throughout. Switching is too confusing for you and your reader.

~Donna Gephart, author of *Olivia Bean, Trivia Queen*

CHAPTER 6

Setting

Nothing sweeps readers away and transports them to another place and time like a well-crafted setting, and this is true not only for novels but also for works of nonfiction. The places we live shape us, just as our early experiences do. Setting is also linked inextricably with plot in both fiction and nonfiction. Imagine how different *The Hunger Games* would be with another setting. Likewise, imagine the Battle of Normandy taking place in the mountains or the desert, rather than at the edge of the sea.

Paying attention to detail and making use of vivid, sensory language are key elements in crafting an authentic setting. In this chapter, we'll practice those skills with some lessons and writing prompts designed to help you spin a sense of place.

In Lesson 27, "Home," guest author Pam Bachorz invites you to remember the place where you grew up in vivid detail and then imagine some changes that might alter your experiences. This is a terrific prompt for helping students imagine the impact that setting has on character development, both for fictional heroes and figures from history.

When we write, our default sense is sight; we tend to describe what we see. Lesson 28, "A Place and Five Senses," challenges writers to expand upon that usual way of seeing to include additional sensory details. By isolating the senses in spurts of writing, teachers can encourage students to consider new details that will enrich their work.

Sometimes, when we're observing for the purpose of recording details, it's useful to imagine looking through different kinds of photographic lenses. In Lesson 29, "The Superpower of Observation," author Gigi Amateau leads us through a writing exercise that challenges us to zoom in to notice specific details and zoom out to see a wider picture. This is a great concept to introduce to students, who may also choose to use a metaphorical zoom lens in writing about history—considering the specific details of a particular event and then zooming out to "see" the larger historical context in which it took place.

In Lesson 30, "Making Sense of Sensory Writing," Donna Gephart shares some examples of sensory language use in mentor texts and encourages us to focus on smell, which has some of the strongest connections to memory.

We turn from smell to sounds in Lesson 31, "Soundtrack of a Place." This lesson is another one with great practical uses for multiple kinds of text. Every place has a soundtrack—a collection of noises—from the quietest hum to the loudest cannon shot. Slowing down to consider the backdrop of sound when writing is an effective way to bring the setting to life, whether that place is a haunted castle shrieking with ghouls, a prehistoric landscape full of dinosaurs, a chemistry lab, or a farmhouse where a former president grew up. What sounds would fill those settings?

Guest author Lisa Schroeder provides more practice in zeroing in on particular senses in Lesson 32, "Smells and Sounds." Using her grandparents' farm as a jumping-off point, she challenges writers to contemplate three places that are part of the setting for their works in progress and focus in on the smells and sounds.

Are you seeing a trend in these lessons? Vivid, sensory details bring settings to life. This chapter should help you make use of these visceral descriptions in your own writing and encourage this same level of description in the work of the young writers for whom you serve as a mentor.

JO'S MORNING WARM-UP

Describe your nighttime routine when you were a little kid. Write the description as if you're writing a scene in a book. Did a parent read to you? What did the voice sound like? What was the book? Did a parent sing to you? What was the song? Did you put yourself to bed? Did you look under your bed or in your closet for monsters? Did you have a special night-light? Did you sleep with a stuffed animal? Did your sheets have pictures on them? What about your pillow? Try to remember as many details as you can.

Jo Knowles is the author of *Read Between the Lines, Living with Jackie Chan, See You at Harry's, Pearl, Jumping Off Swings,* and *Lessons from a Dead Girl*. For more of her Morning Warm-Up prompts, visit www.joknowles.com/prompts.htm.

Lesson 27: Home

By Pam Bachorz

Sometimes, we write best about what we know best, so this prompt shines a spotlight on home. Feel free to explore the prompt on a personal level or as it relates to a work of fiction or nonfiction. For fiction, consider writing from your character's point of view. For writing that explores the content areas, you might try writing as a historical character, animal, plant, rock, or mineral. Exploring the idea of home in a short piece of writing may teach you something about this person, organism, or element that you didn't know before.

TODAY'S ASSIGNMENT

Think of the place that is home for you. It might be where you live today, or perhaps where you grew up. Wherever you choose, be sure to pick a place that you know well. Take one minute to write down every detail about this place that you can think of.

Finished with the first part? Now we're going to twist it around. Take the rest of your time to write about three changes that would make this place utterly altered for you—changes that would mean it was no longer home. What sort of changes? That's entirely up to you. Perhaps you'll change how home looks or smells, or where it's located. Or maybe it's the people there who make it home.

This prompt aims to help you draw rich details from familiar settings into your fiction and to also see how they can be altered to create something entirely different for your stories. Think of it as taking a favorite pair of pants to the tailor and coming home with a pencil skirt!

Pam Bachorz grew up in a small town in the Adirondack foothills, where she participated in every possible performance group and assiduously avoided any threat of athletic activity, unless it involved wearing sequined headpieces and treading water. Pam attended college in Boston and finally decided she was finished after earning four degrees: bachelor's degrees in journalism and environmental science, and master's degrees in library science and business. Pam draws inspiration from the places she knows best: she wrote *Candor* while living in a planned community in Florida, and set *Drought* in the woods where she spent her summers as a child. She lives in the Washington, D.C., area with her husband and their son. Visit her website at www.pambachorz.com/.

Lesson 28: A Place and Five Senses

By Kate Messner

Sight is a dominant sense for most of us, so when we're asked to write a description, visual details usually come to mind first. But true, vivid sensory language in writing needs more than just images. Readers also need to hear the whispers, feel the cold or the roughness, smell the pungent scents, and taste the sweetness in order to experience a place fully. Isolating the senses when brainstorming can help to broaden the sensations, whether you're writing about a fictional setting, an animal's habitat in a piece of nature writing, or a battle or courthouse for a work of nonfiction that relates to history. This is not only a great brainstorming activity but also a great revision tool to share with students when the sensory language or description in a piece has room for improvement.

TODAY'S ASSIGNMENT

Write for two minutes to describe a very specific place. This might be a place you need to describe for a particular work of fiction or nonfiction, or if you're simply free writing, it can be a place that you love, a place you have visited, or a place that frightens you.

Figure 6.1 shows one of my favorite places (which also happens to frighten me sometimes): the Florida Everglades.

FIGURE 6.1
Florida Everglades

Anyplace you choose is fine. If you want to relate this to your work in progress, choose a very specific setting within the piece and imagine yourself there. When your two minutes are up, stop writing.

Now . . . if your place is real and you can go there, do so now. I'll wait . . .

If it's far away, find a picture of it.

If it's not a real place, put yourself there in your mind.

Now write for one minute about *each* of the following:

- Everything you *see*—Pay attention to big things and tiny things. Search for concrete details.
- Everything you *hear*—Be specific. Don't just say "a scraping sound." Say a "high-pitched, raspity-raspity-screeeeeaking noise." You can make up words if you want. If you aren't actually in the place, try to find a video. Or guess what you might hear.
- Everything you *smell*—Especially pay attention to the smells that surprise you. If you're not in the place, pictures can help you smell. Look carefully. What would that dumpster smell like?

- Everything you *feel*—Weather, wind, things that land on you or brush against you. Again, pictures help you imagine if you're not there, and if it's not a real place, try to think of images and then assign sensations from a similar place that might be real (desert, tundra, and so on).

Now go back and rewrite that descriptive paragraph. Include your best tiny, surprising details, and work on senses other than sight. Better? More vivid? This is a fun activity to do with kids, too. Have them write about the playground or gym or cafeteria; then go there and hunt for sensory details.

Lesson 29: Quick-Write: The Superpower of Observation

By Gigi Amateau

As writers, you already know that two of your greatest skills are your strong sense of curiosity and your keen superpower of observation. Curiosity and observation team up to help us understand our thoughts and feelings about the real world; curiosity and observation are the foundation upon which we write new worlds—whether through fiction, poetry, essay, or song. Asking questions, noticing details, and identifying patterns begin inside a writer's heart or mind and then, with practice, make their way down the arm, into the fingertips, and onto the page or screen.

Can we really train ourselves to become more curious? Is observation really a superpower? Absolutely!

To me, the greatest gymnasium or auditorium or home field a writer can use to train and practice is in the natural world. In his little book *Walking*, Henry David Thoreau wrote that "all good things are wild and free." The outdoors is our wild and free writing laboratory—a place to conduct experiments with language and punctuation, a place to explore new territory in our thinking, our feelings, and our storytelling.

TODAY'S ASSIGNMENT

Let's begin by heading outdoors. That's right! Set down your cup of tea and walk outside. Just for a couple of minutes, I promise. If it's nasty out or you're just as snug as a bug, go ahead and practice right where you are.

To get started, shake up your body a bit. Take a quick scan up, down, and all around to notice where you're holding tension or whether you feel stiff. Give those places that are begging for it your permission to relax and a pathway to let go. Roll your shoulders back; now roll your shoulders forward. Inhale. Exhale. And, if that felt good, repeat!

Now look around. Don't alter the way you're watching the world, but notice how you're watching. Chances are that you're focusing on one section of the panorama before you. This is good! As your gaze adjusts to what you're seeing, notice how you slice up the landscape in order to process what you see.

Let's bring a different type of concentration to the act of observing. What happens when you try to take in the whole landscape without focusing on any single image? What changes within your field of vision?

I find that it's difficult to keep panoramic lenses going for very long; I naturally seem to return to observing one piece of the picture. That's okay. Notice when you've lost the wide angle, and simply return to it. A little trick to help if you're having trouble: keep your gaze straight ahead, but bring your peripheral vision into focus. Then, keeping the wide view, go exploring.

As I write this, I'm sitting on the front porch of an antebellum house in Norwood, Virginia, facing the Blue Ridge Mountains. When I practice these magic eyes, I see this place differently than I do when I'm focused on the butterfly bush that drapes the front walkway. Looking out toward the mountain ridge, and taking in the whole panorama, I see a red-tailed hawk riding the current, a dappling of shadow and sunlight across the canopy, a savannah of cumulus clouds against a watery sky, and an old chestnut hound lost in puppy dreams beneath my feet. Each image urges me to turn my glance only upon it, but what else will I see if I keep my wide eyes? The ties of the awning slapping against the porch post, the loop-di-loop of a bumblebee, the zigzag of a dragonfly, an empty white rocker resisting the breeze, and swallows dipping in and out of the treetops down near the river.

Record your own experience with wide-angle watching. What did you observe in your wild and free writer's studio?

Let's switch it up. Which of those images from the landscape would you like to know more intimately?

Form an O with your pointer finger and thumb, as if you were signaling "okay!" Bring the O to one eye and close the other eye. Turn your attention to your subject, and shrink the O by curling your index finger down your thumb toward your palm. Now really examine your subject.

Here's what I see: The dog is not entirely chestnut—only in the darkest places, like the top of her back, the outsides of her thighs, and the points of her ankles. Her belly is almost white. She rests her head under the shade of the bench where I'm sitting. She sleeps with her front and back paws crossed, all ladylike. Her breath rises and falls in an easy cadence. Not even the coal train passing by at the bottom of the hill causes her to stir. The old napper is tired for good reason, I think.

Pollen and leaves and dirt are strewn across her back, her belly, and her haunches. She's been on an adventure today.

Record what you observed with your tiny finger-monocular. Experimenting with different lenses is fun to practice all on its own. You may find a trail of breadcrumbs leading into new ideas or realize that you really enjoy one lens more than the other. You could also use these practices to examine and inform a specific scene of your work in progress by closing your eyes and shifting your mind's eye back and forth between the panoramic and narrow lenses of that scene.

Gigi Amateau is the author of two young adult novels, *Claiming Georgia Tate* and *A Certain Strain of Peculiar*, a Bank Street College Best Children's Book of the Year. She also writes the Horses of the Maury River middle grade series. *Come August, Come Freedom*, her first work of historical fiction, was selected as a Bank Street College Best Children's Book of the Year and a Jefferson Cup honor book. She lives in Richmond, Virginia. Visit her website at www.gigiamateau.com.

Lesson 30: Making Sense of Sensory Writing

By Donna Gephart

Did you know that 80 percent of the brain's energy is used to process what we see? Eighty percent! If you ever want to rest your brain, close your eyes. (But not while driving!)

While writing, we tend to rely mainly on our sense of sight and ignore our other four senses. We should pay attention to all our senses when writing, especially during the most important scenes, the ones we want to slow down for our readers.

Here are examples of writers using sensory description other than sight:

TOUCH: From Holes *by Louis Sachar*

During the summer, the daytime temperature hovers around ninety-five degrees in the shade–if you can find any shade. There's not much shade in a big dry lake.

(Temperature and texture are good ways to use the sense of touch.)

TASTE: From How Lamar's Bad Prank Won a Bubba-Sized Trophy *by Crystal Allen*

. . . to be nice, I take a handful and stuff them in my mouth. Man, these peanuts are off the chain! They're sweet and salty and remind me of Mom's snack mix.

She holds the bowl up. "Take some more, baby. Aren't they good?"

SOUND: From Saint Louis Armstrong Beach *by Brenda Woods*

Almost like a whisper, I heard someone calling out my name. . . . Then, four times in a row, "Saint, Saint, Saint, Saint," each time louder, a girl's voice, until finally she stood right in front of me. "Saint!" she screeched.

SMELL: From Small as an Elephant *by Jennifer Richard Jacobson*

Clothes dryer–that's what the tent smelled like: a trapped-heat smell that filled his nostrils and told him the sun was high.

Smells, in particular, are a powerful way to access memories. The scent of your mother's favorite flower. The odor of your father, after a day's work. The smell of Grandma's soup bubbling on the stove. The sharp stink of a science experiment gone wrong.

TODAY'S ASSIGNMENT

Think of a memory triggered by a smell, sound, taste, or touch, and write about it. Use as many sensory details as you can while writing. Those sensory details will help your readers experience your scene more deeply, and re-create the mood of your memory.

Every time I do this exercise, I'm brought back to my childhood kitchen with my mother cooking at the stove or to our holiday dinners, brimming with aunts, uncles, and cousins, and smells by the dozens. Someone once wrote about the taste of blood and sweat at his local boxing gym. Another young woman wrote about the smell of her school lunchroom, where as a kindergartner, she was made to sit until she finished her lunch. (She sat through every single lunch period—as every grade from kindergarten to eighth sat, ate, and left—before being allowed to leave, her lunch still uneaten.)

Who knows what you will come up with? And who knows where it might lead?

Donna Gephart's humorous writing has appeared on greeting cards, in national magazines, and on refrigerator magnets. Her honors include the Sid Fleischman Humor Award, and her novel *Olivia Bean, Trivia Queen*, about a Jeopardy!-obsessed twelve-year-old, received a starred Kirkus review. See more at www.donnagephart.com.

Lesson 31: Soundtrack of a Place

By Kate Messner

Home has a soundtrack. Other places do, too. And this prompt starts with the sounds of a shopping plaza in Texas (see Figure 6.2).

FIGURE 6.2
Texas birds

When I visited Texas for the first time for a week of school visits in 2012, I couldn't stop noticing all the little things that were different there. The size of the crickets (*enormous!*) and the sounds of the birds (*loud!*). The trees around my hotel swarmed with grackles each night. We have the occasional grackle up north where I live, but certainly not in those numbers, and certainly not at that volume. I mentioned it to one of the librarians hosting my visit, and she seemed surprised. She had barely noticed them. Probably because the birds are part of her everyday soundtrack.

And that got me thinking. All places have a soundtrack, whether that place is a parking lot in Texas or a hospital in London, a grandmother's kitchen in India or a hockey rink in Alberta.

TODAY'S ASSIGNMENT

Write a paragraph or two describing the soundtrack of your place. This can be the place you call home, a place from your memories, or a place in a piece of writing you're working on. Write in your character's voice if you'd like. When you describe the soundtrack, listen for the different levels of sound, too—from the loud honks, to the medium-range notes and voices, to the quiet buzz that underscores everything. What's the soundtrack of your place?

Lesson 32: Smells and Sounds

By Lisa Schroeder

My grandparents lived on a farm, and I spent a lot of time there as a child and a teen. I have lots of wonderful memories, as you can imagine. It wasn't a working farm, but a farm where they had goats to produce milk and keep the grass down and mules to use for their annual hunting trips in eastern Oregon.

There is a special place in my heart for the farm and for my dear grandparents, who are no longer with us, so it's always thrilling when I'm somewhere, not thinking about it at all, and I get a whiff of something that takes me back to that place. Smells have the ability to elicit strong memories. It might happen when our family visits the apple farm every fall or when I'm walking and the air has a certain grassy scent. I'm suddenly back at my grandparents' farm, hanging on to the tire swing that hung from the big, old willow tree.

TODAY'S ASSIGNMENT

Today I'd like you to think about smells and sounds. Adding sensory details is often something writers do as they revise, but here's an exercise you can do anytime, that will help when you're ready to read through your manuscript with an eye on the details. List three places your character visits in your story. For example: school, Grandma's house, and the zoo. Now, with those three places, start brainstorming things your character might smell while there. Get creative! Imagine the people who are nearby as well as what that specific place may smell like. Don't limit yourself to only good smells or only bad smells. Try to find both. At first, you may have trouble describing the scent in detail, and that's okay. Don't edit yourself; just write your thoughts down. When you have a bunch of possibilities, then you can describe the various smells. It's not always easy, I know. You probably won't use the entire list, but one or two good descriptions will add a lot to your scenes.

Also, brainstorm the sounds your character might hear. Make the experience as rich for your reader as it is for your character.

This is a great exercise you can do just about anywhere—take a notebook along when you're taking your kids to an appointment, and work on your lists while you wait.

Lisa Schroeder has written more than a dozen books for kids and teens, including the middle grade series Charmed Life (Scholastic 2014), and the young adult novel *The Bridge from Me to You* (Scholastic 2014). Her books have been translated into several languages and selected for state reading lists. She lives in Oregon with her husband and two sons. Visit her website at www.lisaschroederbooks.com.

Q+A - THE BEST OF Q-AND-A WEDNESDAY: TURNING OFF YOUR INNER EDITOR

We've all heard the saying "The perfect is the enemy of the good," and this is certainly true when it comes to writing. We've all heard the voice of our inner editors, whispering in our ears that what we write isn't good enough, polished enough, fresh enough. What's a writer to do about that?

QUESTION: As a writing teacher and a writer, I sometimes find that my teacher self gets in the way of my writer self. When I write, my teacher self casts doubt over every line and every bend in my writing, and I find that self overanalyzing the writing instead of just allowing it to emerge. So frustrating! I can't seem to be the same nurturing, patient writing coach to my writer self as I am to my own students. Any thoughts?

ANSWERS:

Have you read Stephen King's On Writing? *In it, he talks about writing with the door closed, his process for his first draft where he writes on his own and very quickly, putting down his story as it comes to mind. Set your teacher self outside that door when you write your initial draft. You may surprise your teacher self by what you come up with when you allow her to read it (and help with grammar) later.*

~Joanne Levy, author of *Small Medium at Large*

I think this is how most of us try *to work. But it's hard for me, too. I began as a poet, and that very tight revision method I used for poetry can destroy a novel before I've begun.*

One thought is to try working longhand. The computer makes it so easy to revise as you go. It's much harder with a pen and paper, and so you just keep at it.

~Laurel Snyder, author of *Seven Stories Up* and *Swan: The Life and Dance of Anna Pavlova*

Q+A - THE BEST OF Q-AND-A WEDNESDAY: TOO MUCH DESCRIPTION?

Vivid language brings our settings to life, but is it possible to write too much of a good thing?

QUESTION: I feel like my writing is too descriptive. Is that possible?

ANSWERS:

The easy answer to your question is yes–your writing can be too descriptive. If it bogs down your story or feels like overkill, try paring it down some. I usually have the opposite problem and write very short and bare bones, so I'm probably not the best person to help with how best to edit for that, but the fact that you recognize it is half the battle!

~Joanne Levy, author of *Small Medium at Large*

I would just add that the paring down might come in the revision. If your natural voice is very descriptive, maybe go with it, then walk away from the piece, really give it room and yourself time to forget all your words, and come back to it and read it with a fresh eye. See if you can cut back description that slows the story down and isn't needed. Also, read aloud into a webcam and play it back. Sometimes that is very revealing!

~Gae Polisner, author of *The Pull of Gravity* and *The Summer of Letting Go*

It is possible. While some love the overly descriptive–Dickens, for example–others skim past the wordiness to get to the plot. (He did have an excuse, though; he was paid by the word.)

What you may need to do is to go through each scene, make a list of the different things you describe–in terms of character, setting, and action–or even use different colors to highlight that in the text, and decide what is essential to move your story along.

If there are passages that seem nonessential to you, cut those ruthlessly, but paste them into a separate document. That way, after you've taken a breather, you can reread your story with fresh eyes, see if you miss the description, and reinstate it if you do.

~Jody Feldman, author of *The Seventh Level* and *The Gollywhopper Games*

CHAPTER 7

Plot and Pacing

If you've ever stayed awake reading into the wee hours of the morning, you know how important plot and pacing are in any kind of writing and how writers skilled in this area are able to keep readers turning pages. Quite often, we think of suspense as an element of fiction, but effective writers of nonfiction also understand that building tension and moving things along at a good pace are essential to maintain reader interest.

In this chapter, our guest authors share some effective strategies for plotting a story, whether it's a work of pure fantasy or a true tale from history.

In Lesson 33, "Creating Micro-tension," Lisa Schroeder focuses on ways to create suspense in a story. Readers expect to find tension in the scenes leading up to the climax, but the truth is that to maintain interest, writers must weave tension into every scene.

How do writers create tension and build suspense? Studying an already-published work can provide one of the best educations in plotting and pacing. Lesson 34, "Pacing:

Using a Mentor Text," I take a look at how writers can deconstruct a text that is similar to a work in progress to gain insights about pacing.

Appropriate pacing doesn't always mean speeding things along in a story; sometimes, a writer needs to slow things down to give readers a chance to get to know characters and experience their emotions. In Lesson 35, "Feelings," guest author Lynne Kelly shares the story of how she worked through this issue with her editor and offers thoughts on how writers might take a break from the action to explore characters' emotions.

In fiction, authors must make life difficult for their characters, and in Lesson 36, "Cornering Your Characters," guest author Shutta Crum provides some guidance for how to tighten the noose. This involves considering all of a character's options, not just the first one that comes to mind.

The title of a piece of writing isn't really part of the story line, but it does serve an important role: making a promise to readers about the plot that lies ahead. Lesson 37, "Titles," looks at the challenges involved in choosing a title for your work and offers a hands-on title brainstorming strategy that's great for teacher-writers as well as the students in their classrooms.

Ultimately, the plot and pacing of a piece of writing will determine whether readers are engaged or ambivalent, or whether they rush breathlessly to the end or abandon the piece after a few paragraphs. The strategies in this chapter are useful when it comes to plotting both fiction and nonfiction, to make sure the pace is neither too slow nor too fast and that every page invites a turn to the next.

JO'S MORNING WARM-UP

Suspense and fear are close cousins, so for today's warm-up, describe a fear you had as a child. For an extra challenge, write about that fear from the point of view of your child-self. Or, do this for a main character in a piece you're working on. Go deep.

Jo Knowles is the author of *Read Between the Lines, Living with Jackie Chan, See You at Harry's, Pearl, Jumping Off Swings*, and *Lessons from a Dead Girl*. For more of her Morning Warm-Up prompts, visit www.joknowles.com/prompts.htm.

Lesson 33: Creating Micro-tension

By Lisa Schroeder

You know the drill. When you're writing a story, you have to figure out what your character wants and then put obstacles in his or her way (for example, create conflict) in an effort to create an interesting journey for your readers to follow. Simply put, conflict equals story. Of course, in great stories, there's an internal journey as well as the external one.

So we try our best to focus on the ultimate goal and keep our protagonist reaching for it. But according to agent and author Donald Maass, conflict must be present in small ways, too. In his book *The Fire in Fiction*, he says, "Keeping readers constantly in your grip comes from the steady application of something else altogether: Micro-tension. That is the tension that constantly keeps your reader wondering what will happen, not in the story, but in the next few seconds" (2009, 189).

Did you catch that? "Next few seconds." I don't think enough authors keep this in mind. I'd argue it's even more important when writing for kids and teens, because if they put a book down out of boredom, there's a good chance they won't pick it up again.

So, let's take a look at my middle grade novel *It's Raining Cupcakes*, because it's one I obviously know well. The main character, Isabel, has never been out of Oregon, and she dreams of traveling. That's her goal. But a few things are keeping her dream from coming true. First, she's a kid with limited income. Second, she has a mother who is afraid of flying. And finally, her parents are opening a cupcake shop, so travel is really the last thing they want to do. And yet, Isabel wants to travel. Badly. So she tries to earn money and also enters a baking contest for kids, because the finalists earn a trip to New York City.

In each scene where Isabel is trying to either raise money or come up with a recipe for the baking contest, I tried to create that magical and wonderful micro-tension. Let's look at a couple of examples.

In one scene, Isabel is babysitting three-year-old twins in an effort to earn money. Of course, I let the little boys be boys, so it's fun to read. But I knew I needed more than that to keep the reader engaged. Isabel notices some travel books in the house, and while the kiddie pool is filling up with water, she decides she wants to read those books. She knows it's not wise to leave the boys alone with the water and tries to persuade them to go inside with her, but they refuse. So she tells them to stay out of the water, and off she goes. Here is an example of micro-tension. Suddenly, the reader is nervous. Will the boys get in the pool when Isabel steps away, even though she tells them not to? If they do get in the water, will one of them get hurt? And what if she gets caught?

In another scene, Isabel decides to try out a recipe for the baking contest. Her mom has told her she thinks she should enter a cupcake recipe. After all, if Isabel makes it to the finals, it could be good exposure for the new cupcake shop. But Isabel worries people might think her mom helped her. She really wants to do something different, yet doesn't tell her mom that. One day, while her parents are both out running errands, Isabel attempts a non-cupcake recipe. When Mom and Dad come home earlier than expected, Isabel panics. She grabs the dessert she's just made and without thinking, runs out to the fire escape. Why the fire escape? Because as the author, I knew this was a great way to create some tension. I could have just had them come home and catch her in the kitchen, but why miss out on an opportunity for conflict? Once she's on the fire escape, then what? Does she try to climb down? Does she throw the dessert out on the street? Will her parents catch her out there, hiding from them? And what happens when Isabel realizes she just drank not one, but two root beers, and she suddenly has to go to the bathroom really, really bad? I put Isabel in a pickle, and that's what we must do over and over again in our stories to keep the tension high.

One of the reasons *The Hunger Games* has been so successful, I'd argue, is that Suzanne Collins is a master at creating micro-tension. Think how different the story would have been if it were just Katniss hiding in the woods, all by herself. With every character she encounters, there is tension.

TODAY'S ASSIGNMENT

Write in your journal about how this lesson might be useful with your current work in progress. Ask yourself with each scene what you could do to keep readers on the edge of their seats. Brainstorm a few different things, and then try them out and see how they play out on the page.

Lisa Schroeder has written more than a dozen books for kids and teens, including the middle grade series Charmed Life (Scholastic 2014), and the young adult novel *The Bridge from Me to You* (Scholastic 2014). Her books have been translated into several languages and selected for state reading lists. She lives in Oregon with her husband and two sons. See her website at www.lisaschroederbooks.com.

Lesson 34: Pacing: Using a Mentor Text

By Kate Messner

In the classroom, teachers frequently use a mentor text to introduce students to a particular style of writing. Many share newspaper editorials to introduce students to persuasive writing or invite young writers to create their own poems in the style of Emily Dickinson or Langston Hughes. Mentor texts can be helpful in writing novels as well, particularly when it comes to studying successful pacing.

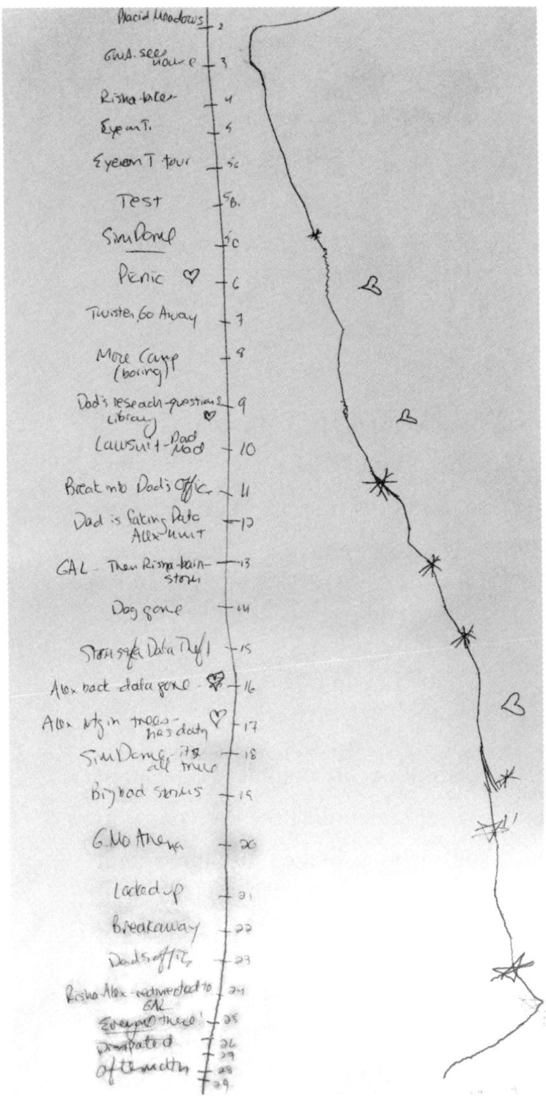

FIGURE 7.1
Plot chart for *Eye of the Storm*

When I was working on my futuristic weather thriller, *Eye of the Storm*, I knew that I wanted the book to move along quickly, with lots of action scenes and suspense. I wanted it to have that "unputdownable" quality that keeps readers turning pages faster and faster. But creating urgency in a story requires careful planning.

As I was revising my novel, I chose to study *The Hunger Games* by Suzanne Collins as a "mentor text" for pacing. I created a classic plot chart—the same kind we use with students when they're analyzing literature, working to identify rising action, climax, and resolution—and I analyzed *The Hunger Games*, chapter by chapter. Where were the high points? The quieter moments? Where were the peaks and valleys in terms of action? When I was finished, I created that same kind of plot chart for my own project (see Figure 7.1).

Mapping it all out on a time line allowed me to see my story's high points and low points, quite literally, and reflecting on the flow of that plot chart allowed me to identify the places where my manuscript might be slowing down and more tension was needed.

TODAY'S ASSIGNMENT

Even if you don't have a completed project right now, try creating a plot diagram to study a book that might be a mentor text for what you'd like to write. If you love quirky fantasies, try mapping the plot of a Roald Dahl favorite. Hoping to write a whodunit? Make a chapter-by-chapter chart for one of your favorite mysteries and take a close look at how the author kept things moving. You'll learn a lot about pacing, and once your own story is complete, you can create another time line/chart to see how closely it fits the pacing map of your mentor text.

Lesson 35: Feelings

By Lynne Kelly

Sometimes, good pacing requires a story to move along more quickly, but it may also call for the author to slow things down a bit. Before my manuscript of *Chained* was submitted to editors, my agent Joanna Volpe asked me to revise. After a while, many of the comments started sounding familiar:

> "And how does he feel about that?"
>
> "How does that make him feel?"
>
> "And he feels . . . ?"

I'd received similar feedback before. Sometimes, the comments on chapters I'd brought to critique meetings showed that readers wanted to see more about how the character was feeling or what they were thinking. A couple of agents who were nice enough to send feedback with the rejection letters indicated the same thing: I wasn't showing enough about what was going on in the character's head. Maybe I was worried about the dreaded "telling" too much instead of "showing." Sure, if I filled the story with internal thoughts like *I was sad,* and *I was so angry,* that would be really boring, but there are ways of showing those feelings that help readers connect with characters more, and thereby root for them, and keep reading the story to see how things turn out.

It took some work to change, because the feelings thing doesn't come naturally for me. Here are a few before-and-after lines, showing how I revised those parts of the manuscript, using Joanna's notes.

Before: I try my best to look brave.

Jo: But inside he feels . . . ?

Me: Um . . . not brave?

Revision: I try my best to look brave, but I worry I'll never feel safe again.

This is from a scene where Hastin surprises his mom with a visit after not seeing her for a couple of weeks, and he notices that her smile seems forced:

Before: I run toward her, then stop. Doesn't she want to see me?

Jo: How does that make him feel? Tie it to his elation, then being deflated in some way.

Revision: I run toward her, then stop. Doesn't she want to see me? All this time, I thought she must be missing me as much as I've missed her, but now it feels like I've done something wrong.

I went through the manuscript and highlighted all the places where I could show Hastin's reaction to what was happening. Then I tackled each highlighted scene by doing a little freewriting about how he felt at that time, and how I'd feel if I were in his place—not just the emotion, but what it would feel like physically, too. Is there a sinking feeling in his stomach? Does he hit something out of anger? Does he feel as if things are so bad, he'll never be happy again? I picked out my favorite words and phrases from the freewriting to add a concise description of the character's feelings to the scene.

TODAY'S ASSIGNMENT

In your own writing, look for places you can show more about how your character is feeling. Think about when you've felt the same way, and free-write about that. Don't worry about overwriting. Get everything on the page first; the editing can come later if you need to scale back. On the surface it might seem as if you don't have much in common with your character, but everyone has at times felt emotions such as fear, loneliness, sadness, or desperation.

After writing, see what you can apply to a scene you're working on. Or, you may want to start a new scene for a new character. Often it takes only one or two strong sentences to make an impact on your readers so they feel what your characters feel.

Lynne Kelly writes contemporary middle grade and young adult fiction. She was born in Galesburg, Illinois, and grew up in the Houston area, where she works as a sign language interpreter. For a few years she also taught special education, a good career for someone with excellent organizational and planning skills. Lacking those skills, she quit teaching in 2006 and now has more time to write. See her website at http://lynnekellybooks.com/wordpress/.

Lesson 36: Cornering Your Characters

By Shutta Crum

Have you ever read one of those books where all along, you're wondering why the main character didn't just . . . call the police, tell a parent (take whatever action any reasonable person would) so that he or she would not be in such a predicament? I can tell you that one of John Grisham's books annoyed me greatly that way. (I won't tell you which title, in case it is one you like.) I simply could not suspend my disbelief. I kept wondering, *Why doesn't the kid just tell everybody, and then the bad guys won't be solely after him to shut him up?*

Authors who don't take care of these kinds of loose ends risk losing readers. A character—especially a main character—must consider and act as any rational person would, unless there is a compelling reason not to do the sensible thing.

If you want to put pressure on your protagonist and pump up the action, you need to corner your "prey," your main character (MC). After all, part of creating plot is putting the hurt on your characters. With every major cause-and-effect link in your plot, you need to be sure to securely close any escape routes. As you do this, you are narrowing the choices of your MC until your MC must make the hard decision you've wanted him or her to make all along. Then you'll have your reader glued to the page.

Let me give you examples from two of my own works. In my teen novel *Spitting Image,* a young girl wants to find out who her father is, and her mother won't talk about him. As it turns out, her mother had been raped. Now, no mother who truly loves her child is going to willingly tell the truth about that. So I had to take away the mother's options and corner her in such a way that she had no choice but to tell her daughter the truth.

In my younger fantasy novel *Thomas and the Dragon Queen*, the whole plot is a simple one of elimination. Thomas starts out on his quest with three things to help him (the traditional armor, sword, and steed). Along the way he gives away, loses, or has stolen from him all the items, including most of his clothes. All of his options as he prepares to do battle with the dragon queen have been slowly stripped away. When he does meet her, he is barefoot and clad in a pair of ragged trousers. There is only one thing he can do—it's a dangerous gamble, and it is precisely what I wanted him to do. He does it, because it is his only remaining choice.

In each novel I write, and in many of my picture books, I have to determine what the "easy outs" are along the way. Then I write scenes that eliminate each alternative logical action. Only then am I able to bring both my MC and my reader to the point where I want them. By using this thinking, I am able to more easily determine what my scenes should be and cut out anything that does not further the plot and character development.

What I recommend is to stop periodically and ask, What are the possible options for my character(s) at this point in the story? (You should do this at least four to six times; more is better.) List the options from the most to the least likely, including the step you want your MC, or other major character, to take. Then make sure you have written scenes that block any other reasonable choices from being made. After all, this process of constantly evaluating our situation and making decisions by eliminating choices is something humans do naturally. You need to do it on behalf of your characters.

TODAY'S ASSIGNMENT

Where are you in your story today? Take a few minutes to list options for your character. What choices does he or she have right now? Which one feels the most realistic?

Shutta Crum writes picture books, novels, and poetry. She is also a storyteller, a public speaker, and a librarian. Her articles about writing have appeared in many professional journals. Her book *Thunder-Boomer!* (Clarion 2009) was chosen by the American Library Association and *Smithsonian* magazine as a Notable Book. *Mine!* (Albert A. Knopf 2011) was listed in the *New York Times* as one of the best board books of the year. Visit her website at http://shutta.com/.

Lesson 37: Titles

By Kate Messner

Whether you're writing a novel, poem, personal narrative, or research paper, consider the title of your piece a promise to readers about the plot that lies ahead.

Titles are sometimes a struggle for me. Even when I think I've found the perfect title for a book, it often finds its way back to me with a note from my editor, asking if we might come up with something a little more vivid, a little more intriguing.

I have a few favorite strategies for coming up with titles. The first is simple. I do a fast-track brainstorming session and force myself to write down at least ten possible titles in two minutes. This time crunch turns off my inner editor, so that title ideas I might have dismissed as stupid or not good enough get scribbled down with all the rest. There's value in this process, because even if the titles aren't perfect, they sometimes spark related ideas that will resonate. Sometimes, one of the ten titles seems to step forward from the crowd and proclaim itself the winner. But not always . . .

When I had finished revising my figure-skating novel, originally called *Sugar on Snow*, I sent it to my editor at Bloomsbury and received the reply I'd been dreading. Perhaps I had some ideas for a new title? I brainstormed until it felt as if there should be smoke coming out of my ears, but I couldn't come up with that perfect combination of words to capture both the main character's love of skating and the novel's rich maple farm setting. So I tried something new.

I scribbled a long list of important and/or vivid words and phrases from the book on a piece of paper, and then I found a pair of scissors. I cut the words apart so that each had its own tiny slip of paper. And I started playing. I mixed up all the slips of paper on my kitchen table, moving them around as if they were magnetic poetry tiles. I experimented with weird combinations, different juxtapositions of words and phrases, until I came up with one I really liked: *Sugar and Ice*. This was a title that captured both the spirit of the ice skating, with all of its sharp competitive edges, and the sweetness of the main character's farm life at home.

TODAY'S ASSIGNMENT

Ready to give your title skills a try? Brainstorm a list of ideas, words, phrases, and images from your project. Come up with as many as possible. Then, use a pair of scissors to cut the paper so each word stands on its own, and begin rearranging. Try making a list of possibilities. At the end of the process, one title will likely ring true, and that's the one you'll add to the top of your page.

Q+A - THE BEST OF Q-AND-A WEDNESDAY: THE PASSAGE OF TIME

If twenty-four hours in the life of a character included every detail that happened in a real person's day, readers wouldn't stick around for long. Experienced writers know that sometimes, it's okay to hit the fast-forward button and move ahead in the story.

QUESTION: I have a question about the passage of time. My middle grade novel in progress takes place over three months. Any advice for how best to skip a week so I don't sound like a play-by-play?

ANSWERS:

One way is to include a non-self-conscious announcement of a day or other fact that indicates that time has passed in between. So, for example, in Summer of Letting Go, *if a chapter took place on* Monday *of the week before the* Fourth of July *and then the next chapter occurred several days later, I started that next chapter something like this: "Saturday, and fireworks pop all day like crazy." We get some sense of several days passing without making a big deal or ticking off stuff. Another way could be to start in the present action a few weeks later, then pepper in some flashbacks of anything that needs to be covered. "Joe and I stand at the pizza parlor eating a pepperoni slice. Five days ago, I was talking to* Maddy *and only dreaming Joe might ask me out." That description lets the reader know time passed, and then you could toss in a scene with the character and Maddy, trying to instigate the call with Joe or whatever. I think you get the gist.*

~Gae Polisner, author of *The Pull of Gravity* and *The Summer of Letting Go*

I have a lot of time shifts in my books. A couple of ways you can handle them are to have your characters discuss what happened or to have an incident happen during which your characters can refer to what occurred in the past.

~Margo Sorenson, author of *Spaghetti Smiles* and *Time of Honor*

CHAPTER 8

Flowing Between Nonfiction and Fiction: Finding the Story

Writing skills and strategies transcend genre and form. The skills that make you a better writer of realistic fiction can also make you a stronger poet, and the strategies that help you craft riveting science fiction are the same tactics that you might use to write engaging nonfiction. Research, after all, is essential for almost all types of writing. It comes to mind first in the area of nonfiction, but writers of historical and realistic fiction, science fiction, and fantasy find themselves searching for real-world details to bring a scene to life.

The guest authors who contributed to this chapter write a diverse range of books, but they share two qualities, almost universally. The first is a patient attention to details, to get things just right. The second is a passionate curiosity for their subjects, one that readers can't help but find infectious.

In Lesson 38, "Beyond the Textbook," Sarah Albee challenges us to use a different sort of mentor text. In this case, the classic (and sometimes boring) social studies textbook becomes a guide for how *not* to write engaging stories from history. Instead, Albee urges writers to dig deeper, find the flesh-and-blood people from the stories, and explore their messy, authentic lives in more detail.

Guest author A. J. Paquette shines a light on "Research and Science Fiction" in Lesson 39, using her novel *Paradox* as an example. Just because a piece of writing is science fiction doesn't mean that all sense of reality needs to go out the window. As they ask questions and research the answers, writers bring authenticity to their work, whether those stories are out of this world or solidly grounded on Earth.

Ask any student, and he or she will tell you that field trips are always a highlight of the school year, so it's no surprise that authors love their field trips as well. In Lesson 40, "Write What You Want to Know," Pamela Voelkel shares the story of her family's travel to research the Jaguar Stones book series and offers some suggestions for gathering lively details even when it's not possible to make a trip in person.

Humans are visual creatures, so depending on the type of writing you're doing, adding images may bring a lot more intrigue to the text. In Lesson 41, "Research and Images," Sarah Albee shares her motivations for including numerous images in her work along with some strategies for finding those images and seeking permission to share them.

In Lesson 42, "When the Story Only *You* Can Write Is Someone Else's Story," Laurel Snyder shares the inspiration behind her picture book biography, *Swan: The Life and Dance of Anna Pavlova*, along with the process she and her editor went through as they boiled down heaps of biographical information to a focused, heartfelt story about a dancer who reached out to the world. Laurel also offers thoughts on planning a biography with a focus and an emotional heart.

Many teachers who write make use of their own classrooms for inspiration. In Lesson 43, "Writing Where You Are," Donalyn Miller shares her classroom-based writing story. With a list of questions as writing prompts, she invites fellow teacher-writers to reflect on their own classrooms, students, and practice to consider the threads that emerge and where they might lead.

Our passions are frequently the best story starters. In Lesson 44, "Obsessions, Volcanoes, and Story Structure in Nonfiction," Elizabeth Rusch invites us back in time to her childhood to watch the eruption of Mount St. Helens in 1980, which inspired her to write numerous books. Liz shares her process for choosing a structure for works of nonfiction and leads writers through a series of questions designed to prompt stories that are unique and engaging.

JO'S MORNING WARM-UP

Begin with the words *It all started when . . .* and keep writing. I think this could be a helpful exercise, too, for when you're trying to figure out where your project really starts.

Jo Knowles is the author of *Read Between the Lines, Living with Jackie Chan, See You at Harry's, Pearl, Jumping Off Swings,* and *Lessons from a Dead Girl*. For more of her Morning Warm-Up prompts, visit www.joknowles.com/prompts.htm.

Lesson 38: Beyond the Textbook

By Sarah Albee

Everyone loves amazing-but-true stories. Hollywood producers know this. Theatergoers flock to movies based on historical events, such as *Titanic*, *The Great Escape*, *Gandhi*, *Schindler's List*, and *Apollo 13*. Great writers know this, too. From Homer to Shakespeare to Dickens to Harper Lee to Laurie Halse Anderson, they've kept their readers spellbound with stories based on real people and events. History can be enthralling, compelling, suspenseful, and engaging, full of stories that appeal to people at an emotional level.

But the history you read in textbooks is almost never that. Find a middle school kid, any middle school kid, and ask her to tell you her least-favorite subject. More often than not, the answer is going to be social studies/history. It's boring, the kid will tell you. It's irrelevant. The textbook weighs a ton, and the reading is deadly dull.

Let's examine the reasons why social studies and history textbooks—I'll call them anti-mentor texts—are so off-putting. The textbooks kids read today aren't all that different from the ones I had in school growing up. The revised editions my own kids have on their shelves are bigger, glossier, heavier, and more graphically distracting, but the text is still the same dull, orderly, bland narrative, full of barely connected facts and fragmented episodes boiled down to noncontroversial material that is meant to offend no one. The end-of-chapter questions are either impossibly broad, reductive, boring, or all three. Teachers are often under pressure to "teach to the test," and the tests are often multiple-choice assessments imposed on them by the districts/forces outside their classrooms, so kids memorize the facts, and then they forget them as soon as the test is over.

As a writer of history books for kids, my mission is to try to mitigate the damage done by textbooks and multiple-choice testing, to make kids un-think that they hate history, to show them how fascinating history can be. I like to do this by selecting one subject kids will be interested in—be it sanitation, insects, clothing, disease, or dentistry—and tracing it chronologically through history. I can't, nor do I wish to, cover everything. Mine is a selective view of world history, but history is always a series of choices made by the writer about what to include and what to leave out.

Ask any writer, or any good teacher of writing, what makes a good story, and the answer will usually involve words such as *tension* and *conflict*. To generate tension, a good writer or teacher knows you have to omit inessential details. A writer of thrillers might say his character made a cup of tea, but he wouldn't give us a step-by-step description of his character filling the teakettle, turning on the flame, taking down the tea cup, choosing tea, and so on. All those details would bore the reader. Nor do we want to read a story about a contented person to whom nothing bad happens, who has no high-stakes choices to make, who doesn't change. Stories, good stories, have just the right amount of detail to keep readers interested; they are full of tension, emotion, pathos.

So what's a teacher to do? My hope is that teachers may complement the textbook with nonfiction books written for kids. Include biographies and fascinating narratives of specific historical events. Teachers can also help their students read the textbook with a critical eye, asking questions such as, Is this accurate? A partial truth? Are there crucial omissions? Is there another point of view? History is full of conflict, tension, controversy, emotion, and drama—in short, all the things that make a great story.

TODAY'S ASSIGNMENT

Flip through a history textbook. What story is glossed over, begging to be explored in more depth? Spend a little time brainstorming about how you might go beyond the textbook to tell a more dramatic, interesting story from history.

Sarah Albee is the author of *Bugged: How Insects Changed History* and *Poop Happened: A History of the World from the Bottom Up*. This immediately tells you that (a) she is a history and science geek, and (b) she has a great sense of humor. Visit her website at www.sarahalbeebooks.com.

Lesson 39: Research and Science Fiction

By A. J. Paquette

I am known for reading widely in all kinds of genres, but one that I always come back to, and consistently find a vast enjoyment in, is science fiction. However, I have recently come to learn in an entirely new way that there is a huge difference between *reading* science fiction and *writing* it.

On some level, of course, this is obvious. It's also true of any book, any genre. But I think in my case, when I began writing my YA science fiction novel, *Paradox*, I didn't fully realize just *how* science-intensive it would end up being. The story seed began in my mind with the main character, Ana, who awoke confined in a small room without any memories or knowledge of who or where she was. As the plot came together and the backstory unfolded, I quickly determined that the small space was the inside of a rocket; that Ana was on a far-off, habitable planet; and that she had an unknown mission to accomplish and a limited time to do so.

All well and good. The story begins, and the plot grows from there. All stories tend to do this, and I'm certainly no stranger to the accompanying research process. My first novel, *Nowhere Girl*, is set in Thailand, a country I've visited several times, but I still had to do vast amounts of research about motorcycle taxis, boat rides along the Chao Phraya River, best travel routes from Chiang Mai to Bangkok, and much more.

But when I began delving into *Paradox*, I found that there were new levels of research needed. Despite my having needed to brush up on many aspects of everyday life in modern Thailand when writing *Nowhere Girl*, I had a certain foundation to draw from: I had *been* to Thailand. I had a basic sense of the culture and country. I never had set foot, however, on the planet Paradox. I haven't traveled by rocket ship. I have never analyzed contagious diseases or personally watched someone near me die a cripplingly horrible death.

Confession time: At first, I looked for shortcuts. I'm used to writing first, researching second. I return to my first drafts armed with facts and figures and proceed to layer in details, shifting the plot around any factual roadblocks that require the story to move in a different direction. With *Paradox*, as my editor gently pointed out to me, I needed to do my research first. I needed to know all there was to know about planet rotation in a binary solar system. I had to chart the symptoms of how my disease works, how it is spread, and how it might be cured. And this kind of research, at least for this particular writer, did not come easy.

I spent hours online. I pored over books from as many libraries as I could access. I looked up experts and phoned them. I was lucky enough to have several family members and friends with specialties in the areas my book required, and I shamelessly begged their expertise, which they were all happy to share. Armed with this information, I wrote scientific memos. I composed newspaper articles. I drew diagrams of how the suns would rise and set across the planet Paradox.

It wasn't always fun. I distinctly remember telling a friend that if I ever decided to write another science fiction book in the future, to please punch me in the face. But looking at it now in hindsight, I feel immensely satisfied for having gone so deeply into a project.

It's important that I add a caveat here: Despite my best efforts at research and fact-finding, I am *not* by any stretch of the imagination a scientist. Although I did have several scientist friends review the various elements and backdrops, and while my goal and hope was to get it as scientifically accurate (within its futuristic sphere) as possible, I'm fully aware of my own limitations in that area.

My hope is that I've crafted a world that is rich in detail and scientific potential. At best, I hope I've created memorable characters in a story that will draw in young readers and maybe excite their own scientific curiosity. At worst . . . well, if nothing else, I hope I've written a rip-roaring good story, so that readers will be too busy flipping the pages to notice any of the writerly lacks that must exist within any story.

TODAY'S ASSIGNMENT

Flip through a science magazine or website such as *Popular Science* or *Scientific American*. What article or feature captures your imagination and might provide the seed for a work of science fiction? Spend a little time brainstorming ideas and research questions that might need to be answered along the way.

Ammi-Joan (A. J.) Paquette spent her formative years moving from place to place, which left her with an insatiable curiosity about the wide world and everything in it. A voracious reader since early childhood, she's thrilled to now be able to share her stories with readers everywhere. She lives outside of Boston, where she balances her own writing and her day job as a literary agent. Visit her website at www.ajpaquette.com.

Lesson 40: Write What You Want to Know

By Pamela Voelkel

The worst advice I was ever given was "Write what you know." Those four little words gave me a twenty-year writer's block. It was only when I'd spent half my life as an advertising copywriter that the truth hit me. If I didn't want to write about what I knew, all I had to do was know about something else.

So when my husband, Jon, started writing adventure stories based on his childhood in South and Central America, I joined him on the project. At first, my stories were just ripping yarns, with some cool Maya pyramids in the background for local color. But as we started to read about the Maya, we discovered that their story was more amazing than anything we could make up. We also discovered that many of the books in print were out of date. That's when we decided to turn our website into a portal for teachers to access the latest research into the Maya, and to offer free lesson plan CDs.

Time was passing. Jon had completed a course at Harvard on reading and writing Maya glyphs, but I was still struggling with writing English. I was concerned that I couldn't describe the sights and sounds of the jungle if I'd never been there, so when I saw an ad for a cheap flight to Belize, I convinced Jon that we had to go. Not just us; we also needed to take our three children—then ages two, nine, and twelve—to observe their reactions to spooky pyramids and creepy-crawlies and whatever else might await us.

After that, we traveled to the area every year. It was our second trip that changed everything. We were at a remote site in Guatemala, on a day when locals got free entry. Our son is very tall, and he attracted a crowd of local youths who followed him around, giggling and taking pictures of him. Our tour guide watched this for a while, then puffed out his chest and stepped forward. "Remember these people," he said in Spanish, "but not because their son is tall. Remember them because they are writing books about the Maya, and thanks to them, children in North America will be reading about your history and culture." There was a moment of silence. Then these hoodie-wearing, gum-chewing Guatemalan teenagers burst into applause, with the ancient pyramids right there behind them. My heart sank into my jungle boots. Now we had a responsibility to these kids. Now we would have to tell the story of the modern Maya as well. And that's where our lead character (and everyone's favorite), Lola the Maya girl, came from.

When it's not possible to board an airplane bound for your research destination, writers can find plenty of virtual travel opportunities online. Google Maps and Google Earth have satellite images and photographs that will show you the view from many addresses all over the world. YouTube, too, has videos that writers can use for virtual visits when a real one might not be possible.

Give it a try with your own writing today. Find a video or street-view map or a collection of images of your setting online. Check it out and take some notes, paying attention not only to what you see, but also what you hear, what you might feel, and what you imagine it would smell like. How would your characters see that place?

Pamela and Jon Voelkel write the Jaguar Stones books set in Latin America, *Middleworld* and *The End of the World Club*. Visit the series website at www.jaguarstones.com.

Lesson 41: Research and Images

By Sarah Albee

As a writer of historical nonfiction, I made a shrewd career move: I married a history teacher. I have learned a lot from my husband about how to make history fun, interesting, and relevant. My goal as a writer is close to his goal as a teacher: to reach that ever-elusive group of kids who think they don't like history, and to get them excited about it.

There will always be self-motivated, naturally curious students who are born loving history, but by the time they land in high school classrooms, the vast majority of kids have decided that history is boring. These are the kids my husband has to win over. As a middle grade writer, my goal is to start converting them earlier.

I'm constantly scheming up ways to snag the attention of a reluctant reader, to get him or her to open my book or read my history blog. I try to approach my topic from an offbeat angle, like the history of how civilizations from the Stone Age to the present have dealt with their waste or how bugs have affected human history.

I also try to use humor wherever possible. Kids of all ages love to laugh. Maybe this approach stems from the nine years I spent working for *Sesame Street*. We subversively disguised our preschool teaching curriculum in the form of game shows, television commercials, silly songs, and parodies. (My book *Brought to You by the Letter B!* is still one of my proudest achievements.)

But my most effective attention-grabbing strategy is to use visuals to enhance my topic. I'm constantly asking myself, What makes a compelling picture? What will draw kids into the book? On my blog, I like to lead with the coolest picture I can find. My posts include photos relating to everything from what babies used to wear (www.sarahalbeebooks.com/2012/06/how-they-rolled) to the way little boys were once forced to wear dresses (www.sarahalbeebooks.com/2012/06/boys-will-be-boys-eventually/).

Do pictures catch your eye? Snag your interest? Let's face it: Like it or not, as writers, we're also salespeople. We're luring readers toward our writing. And kids these days are savvy consumers. As teachers, you know better than anyone that there's a lot of competition out there calling for their attention.

That's the challenge—and the fun—of using pictures to enhance your writing. And one of the best parts of being a nonfiction writer is that we writers get to play a big role in choosing the pictures that will accompany our text.

I absolutely love finding images. Sometimes you can acquire a picture just by asking. Figure 8.1 shows a "zombie bee," a phorid fly parasitizing a honeybee. The photo was snapped by Chris Quock, an undergraduate at the University of Southern California. I tracked down Chris by contacting his professor, and Chris then sent me his picture to include in my book (and later gave permission for it to be included in this one!).

FIGURE 8.1
Zombie bee (Photo by Christopher Quock)

Many public domain images are digitized and available to download from online sites. But it can be even more fun to find pictures yourself. I took a research trip to Washington, D.C., where I visited the "still pictures" divisions at both the National Archives and the Library of Congress. It's such a thrill to find a photo that has never before been published. It can take hours to find that one picture, but it's worth it.

Sarah Albee is the author of *Bugged: How Insects Changed History* and *Poop Happened: A History of the World from the Bottom Up*. This immediately tells you that (a) she is a history and science geek, and (b) she has a great sense of humor. Visit her website at www.sarahalbeebooks.com.

Lesson 42: When the Story Only You Can Write Is Someone Else's Story

By Laurel Snyder

I never planned to write a biography. It was an accident. Honestly, I've always been intimidated by nonfiction and the idea of trying to "get it right." As an author and poet, it's much easier for me to make things up than to fact-check. But when I went looking for a picture book about the Russian dancer Anna Pavlova for a ballet-loving young friend of mine, and couldn't find one, I felt a need to write one.

My eight-year-old self would never have forgiven me if I hadn't at least tried.

You see, Pavlova was an obsession for me when I was a kid. I photocopied pictures of her to hang on my walls. Once, in fourth grade, I did a math project about her, using photographs of her legs and arms, mid-dance, to show a variety of angles and to explain concepts such as symmetry. My favorite book for many years was an old coffee-table photo book, translated from Russian and long out of print, that included pages from Pavlova's own diaries.

So when I realized that young dancers today had no such book to reference, I decided to write one, but I wasn't exactly sure how to begin, or where. I dug out my old photo book for the first time in decades, looking for inspiration, and was tickled to find I'd scribbled notes in the margins with a pencil. "Someday I will dance as no one has ever danced . . . I will be Pavlova's twin!"

As silly as that sounds, it actually became my point of entry for the book. My own love for Pavlova became part of my subject. You see, the problem wasn't that I couldn't find anything to write about. Pavlova's life was rich with historical details, and those details would have made a fine book without any other treatment. She danced for the last czar of Russia, and then found herself an expatriate when the revolution came. She lived through world wars and founded an orphanage for war refugees. She kept swans as pets! Frothy desserts are named after her!

But somehow, those details didn't feel like enough. They didn't feel like a *reason* for a book, and they didn't begin to explain the way I *felt* about Pavlova as a kid. Staring at my scribbles, I realized that the story I wanted to tell wasn't just about Pavlova and the details of her life. It had to do with the kids I was writing the book for, devoted young dancers like I had been: girls (and boys too) a century after Pavlova who wanted to grow up to wear feathery swan dresses just like her. I decided to enter the story in the very same place I'd left it—as a young dancer.

Wonderfully, the more I researched Pavlova's life, the more I found concrete support for my deeply emotional impulse. It turned out that Pavlova hadn't just inspired me as a kid because she was an amazing dancer, and beautiful. In fact, Pavlova had been a sort of missionary for ballet during her life, in an era when few people besides wealthy Europeans had seen that kind of dance performed.

I talked to my editor, in a series of very excited emails, and we chatted on the phone. She agreed that we should structure the book to reflect Pavlova's generosity, her need to share the ballet she loved so much. This meant we'd need to include Pavlova's travels to developing nations, as well as her trick of throwing *back* the flowers people tossed to her at the end of a performance.

Of course, I still had lots of work to do. Crafting the language and triple-checking the details took time. And while I ended up incorporating some interesting events from Pavlova's life, I also lost some really neat historical details when I decided to sculpt this particular narrative. For instance, it turned out that Pavlova was instrumental in the development of contemporary toe shoes, but the scene in which I tried to tell that story (describing her as a cobbler, an elf in the night, hammering at her own shoes, and how the other kids picked on her for it) seemed to distract from the core idea of her generosity, so we cut it.

One thing that felt important to me in writing this book was including Pavlova's death. I'm always surprised at how often death is left out of picture book biographies, as though children don't grasp that someone who lived a century ago is dead. In Pavlova's case, the death scene was especially moving, and I was committed to keeping it. Her generosity and her legacy made her death feel even more meaningful, as though it wasn't just an ending, but a beginning, because her work would ripple through the decades and centuries to find its way into the lives of children for generations to come.

Now I'm trying to write another picture book biography, in the same spirit, and I'm struggling to find the emotional charge, the core idea. I think it's very possible I won't succeed in writing this book. The emotional connection is a critical piece for me. I don't have any real interest in simply relating someone's life story. As an author, I need to find a thread from the subject's life to my own if I'm to take on his or her story and feel justified in telling it.

When conducting writing workshops, I tell kids all the time that they need to hunt for the stories that only *they* can write. Typically, I say this in relation to fiction, to invention. I'm trying to help my students craft the details of their own lives and blend them into their imaginary landscapes. But I'm realizing now that the challenge is no different when a writer is working on nonfiction.

I don't think it's enough to ask, Whose story *can* I tell? Rather, I need to ask myself, Whose story *should* I tell? I believe I need to earn the right to describe someone else's life, by knowing that person and connecting with him or her in a distinctive way.

TODAY'S ASSIGNMENT

Write about someone from history whose life interests you. What are the most fascinating details that come to the surface? If you were to write a biography of this person, how would you frame the emotional heart of the book?

Laurel Snyder is the author of many books for kids, including five novels: *Bigger than a Bread Box, Seven Stories Up, Any Which Wall, Penny Dreadful,* and *Up and Down the Scratchy Mountains OR The Search for a Suitable Princess.* She also writes picture books, among them *Baxter, the Pig Who Wanted to Be Kosher,* and *SWAN: The Life and Dance of Anna Pavlova.* Laurel lives in Atlanta. Visit her website at http://laurelsnyder.com.

Lesson 43: Writing Where You Are: Professional Writing for Teachers

By Donalyn Miller

When I was a kid, writing well was part of the school game. I never wrote outside of school. I was told that I was a good writer. I earned high grades on my writing from teachers—the only audience who saw my writing. In high school, I wrote my assignments in the car on my way to school while my best friend, Larry, navigated his Ford Pinto around potholes. I dodged my English teachers when they asked for my rough drafts. I never wrote any; it seemed like a waste of time. I don't think I was ever taught how to write. I was a student of what my fellow Texan Gretchen Bernabei calls the "Ass/Ass" method of writing instruction: assign the writing, and then assess it. For me, writing was an obstacle course of grammar, mechanics, and formatting. I wrote the papers my teachers assigned, earned my A, and gave my papers to my mom to hang on the fridge.

Even after I became a language arts teacher, I didn't write outside of school. I wrote in front of my students as a model—because my mentors told me I was supposed to—but that was it. Writing for the sake of writing held no relevance for me. I didn't have a clue about how to teach writing. I knew that something was missing, and I was at a complete loss to figure out what it was.

During my fifth year of teaching, I enrolled in graduate school. Every week that fall, I sat with colleagues Audrey Wilson and Jennifer Isgitt, listening to them talk about the National Writing Project and how much it had changed their professional lives. The fire I saw in their eyes when they talked about what they had learned about writing and teaching during the Summer Institute compelled me. I wanted that fire, too. I applied to the Writing Project that spring. I wasn't entirely sure what I was getting myself into, but I didn't care. I only wanted to be a better writing teacher.

That summer, surrounded by other teachers as we wrote and shared our stories, I finally understood that to be a better writing teacher I needed to write. I began keeping a notebook and jotting poems and essays about my daughters. When school started, I recorded anecdotes about my students and our days together as readers and writers, too. Showing my real writing efforts to my students terrified me, but I discovered that sharing my writing life with my students helped them write better. Writing outside of school for the first time, I began to see myself as a writer.

Early that school year, I received a call from Elizabeth Rich, an editor at *Teacher Magazine*. Elizabeth had worked with my principal, Ron Myers, a few years before and contacted him to see if he had any teachers who could write a one-shot Ask the Mentor column for the magazine. Ron told her, "I have one."

After introducing herself, Elizabeth asked, "I hear that your students read fifty books a year without any rewards or incentives. Is that true?"

I replied, "Isn't reading its own reward?"

She responded, "Well, how do you do it?"

Put on the spot, I realized that this was not an easy question to answer. "I don't know. It's like I'm some sort of whisperer. I talk to the kids about books and they read them."

The moniker "The Book Whisperer" stuck, as did Elizabeth's original question, How do you do it? Through my writing, I have been trying to answer that question ever since—both for myself and for the people who read my writing. That first Ask the Mentor column turned into three. *Teacher Magazine* invited me to write a blog. I remember thinking at the time, "I won't tell them that I don't know the first thing about blogging." When several publishers approached me about writing a book, I thought, *I wonder how long it will take them to figure out that I am not a writer.* Whenever I receive an invitation to submit an article or write a blog post, it still surprises me. Don't they know that I am still trying to figure out how to be a good writer? Don't they know that I struggle with writing and hate it some days?

Dorothy Parker famously said, "I hate writing, I love having written." I relate. I do. Discovering that I am able, in spite of crushing insecurity and my complete lack of discipline, to write something worthy amazes me.

I think it is okay to admit when we have a love/hate relationship with writing. The most important thing is to keep writing. We are writers because we write—nothing more, nothing less.

Penny Kittle talks about Writing Territories, topics that writers revisit again and again. My territories include my daughters, my love for nature, and my childhood stories. Mostly, I write about my students and our shared lives as readers and writers. As teacher-writers, recording our classroom stories can be a great place to start writing. For teachers, writing about our classrooms is the ultimate reflective practice—we see how our daily interactions and observations inform our thinking about teaching and learning. We also capture our remarkable students, their experiences, and how they shape our lives.

TODAY'S ASSIGNMENT

Think about your classroom and your students. What moments stick with you? Record your daily anecdotes in your notebook. Start with what happens in your classroom each day. What did your students say and do? How did you respond or feel about what happened? What did you notice that was funny or insightful or poignant? After recording an event as well as you can, dig deeper into what this moment reveals about your teaching and your interactions with your students. Did this moment move your students forward somehow? What did you learn? How did this moment build community among your students and you? What did you discover about your students that you didn't know?

Look back through your school stories occasionally to see what threads or overarching themes emerge. Perhaps you can shape your anecdotes into an article and submit it to a professional journal. Is there a particular student you write about often? Perhaps this child can be the protagonist in a fictional story. For every teacher, our classroom stories provide powerful writing territory that fuels our writing and our teaching.

Donalyn Miller has worked with a wide variety of upper elementary and middle school students. In her book *The Book Whisperer*, Donalyn reflects on her journey to become a reading teacher and describes how she inspires and motivates her middle school students to read forty or more books a year. In *Reading in the Wild*, Donalyn collects responses from nine hundred adult readers and uses this information to teach lifelong reading habits to her students. Donalyn facilitates the community blog *The Nerdy Book Club*, and co-writes a monthly column for Scholastic's *Principal-to-Principal Newsletter*. Visit her website at http://bookwhisperer.com/.

Lesson 44: Obsessions, Volcanoes, and Story Structure in Nonfiction

By Elizabeth Rusch

My obsession with volcanoes began in May 1980, when I was a kid watching footage of Mount St. Helens erupting. I was awestruck by the huge gray-black plume of ash pumping high into the sky. Still, volcanoes seemed distant and almost foreign to me until I moved to Portland, Oregon, where Cascades volcanoes, including St. Helens, loom at the skyline. For a while, volcanoes were my playground, where I could hike, camp, and ski.

Then in 2004, Mount St. Helens rumbled back to life. From my neighborhood I could see it spitting steam high into the sky. The volcano began building a new dome, pumping out lava fast enough to fill a bedroom in about a minute.

I drove up to the Mount St. Helens National Volcanic Monument with my son for a closer look. While we watched a plume rise from the crater before us, a ranger handed my son a rock. "This rock was born yesterday," he said. A rock born yesterday! A scientist had taken a lava sample from the crater the day before—and when he handed it to the ranger, it was still warm from the heat inside the Earth.

I knew then that I wanted to write a book about volcanoes, but I had no idea that I would write three books.

At first, I wasn't sure what to write. After all, library and bookstore shelves are full of volcano books. So, I started my research by reading them all. As I read, I noticed something. The vast majority of the books were almost formulaic in their presentation. The cover generally featured a volcano spewing red-hot lava. Early sections described a famous violent eruption. Middle sections gave the science of volcanoes, including discussions of the Earth's layers, plate tectonics, the Ring of Fire, the connection between earthquakes and volcanoes, and how magma moves in an eruption. Only a handful, all out of date, focused on Mount St. Helens. None covered cutting-edge volcano monitoring science or told the dramatic story of Mount St. Helens's recent eruption and how it had built a new dome higher than the Empire State Building.

I have been a magazine writer for a long time, so I continued my research by interviewing volcanologists who study Mount St. Helens. They all mentioned that when the volcano began to rumble to life, it was a great mystery whether or not it would actually erupt. After the third or so interview, an idea began to take shape: What if I wrote a book that showed how volcano monitoring is like detective work? As I continued interviewing volcanologists, I asked them about the parallels: When they are worried that a volcano might erupt, what clues do they look for? What gadgets do they use? I asked them to recount how the 2004 eruption unfolded, what evidence they collected, and what they thought about the evidence. I asked, What clues were distracting, confusing, or misleading? What did they predict would happen each step of the way, and were they right or wrong?

After finishing and transcribing hours of interviews, I wrote an outline. I decided I would introduce Mount St. Helens as "the suspect," with aliases and prior offenses. Each of the next chapters would focus on one clue that volcanologists gather (such as earthquake clues, gas clues, and heat clues). Each chapter would end with a real case study from Mount St. Helens's 2004–2008 eruption where kids could apply what they learned about the clue to guess what Mount St. Helens might do next. "Case Closed" sections would tell what actually happened each step of the way. I made a list of sidebars I wanted to include that would allow me to cover the background science and instruments without distracting from the detective narrative.

With this concept and outline in place, I sorted through my notes, curating the best anecdotes, quotations, and details to tell this story. The result was my first volcano book, *Will It Blow? Become a Volcano Detective at Mount St. Helens* (Sasquatch Books 2007).

As I was researching and writing *Will It Blow?*, I learned some things that made me think that there were other important aspects of volcanology that had not been covered yet—stories that I thought needed to be told. For one thing, I learned that powerful, destructive eruptions featured on almost all the book covers were not the most common kind of eruption. Two-thirds of all volcanic eruptions are relatively peaceful dome-building eruptions, like the 2004–2008 eruption of Mount St. Helens. This type of eruption has transformed our landscapes, building mountains and creating islands where there were none before.

Focusing on the creative force of volcanoes seemed to be the perfect way to introduce volcanoes and volcano science to very young children. Again, I had a basic concept: the creative force of volcanoes. Next I needed a structure. I decided I would introduce the concept, explain it, and then give vivid examples. I spent a lot of time reading about recent and historic dome-building eruptions, from a volcano that suddenly sprang up in a Mexican field, to ones that grew underwater or under glaciers. I wanted a rich variety of examples that kids would find fascinating. Working with my editor at Charlesbridge, we decided on a thirty-two-page picture book format for *Volcano Rising*, with two layers of text. In the main layer of text, I employed lyrical language so that it's lovely to read aloud to kids ages three and up. The second layer offers more detailed descriptions of fascinating creative eruptions for parents or teachers to share with very young kids or for independent readers to explore on their own.

The idea for the third book emerged from a problem I faced researching *Will It Blow?* I had a very hard time setting up an interview with one of the volcanologists, John Pallister, who everyone told me was the best person to talk with about rock and lava clues (and who probably harvested that lava sample that my son held at the visitor center). When John and I finally sat down for the interview, he apologized for being so difficult to reach. He explained that he headed a group called the Volcano Disaster Assistance Program, a small group of American volcanologists who offer assistance in volcano crises all around the world to help predict eruptions so governments can get people out of harm's way. *Wow*, I thought. *That would make an amazing book.*

Some years after writing *Will It Blow?*, I contacted John and developed a proposal to write a Scientists in the Field series book on VDAP for Houghton Mifflin Harcourt. The proposal helped me begin thinking about the structure. As I did background reading, I knew that I wanted to write about the eruption of Nevado del Ruiz, which killed twenty-three thousand people and spurred the creation of VDAP. I also wanted to include the 1991 eruption of Mount Pinatubo in the Philippines, where the volcanologists really showed how they could use science to save lives. And then I wanted to write about recent work. But what exactly that would be would be dictated by the volcanoes themselves.

I began reading and interviewing scientists involved in the two historical eruptions. I wanted to be able to re-create those experiences for readers so they unfold before them. I set up a time to shadow some Chilean volcanologists who were training with VDAP on Mount St. Helens. Finally, John generously invited me and the photographer to Mount Merapi, in Indonesia, which had erupted violently in fall 2010. Before we left, I asked John and others to recount their experiences, so I could re-create that eruption. While on location, I frantically took notes as the scientists poked around in steaming fields and mounds of ash, and peppered the American and Indonesian volcanologists, the villagers, the volcano evacuation refugees, and the local volcano observers with questions about their experiences.

When I returned and began to write, I was overwhelmed with material. I had to ask myself, What is this book really about? I decided that it needed to be a no-holds-barred immersion into the destructive power of volcanoes and the intense scientific challenge of predicting deadly violent eruptions. It was a story of struggle, to predict eruptions and prevent tragedies, in difficult circumstances and against all odds. And it was about people: the American and international scientists who monitor the volcanoes and the people who live on the flanks of these ticking bombs. Choosing that lens helped me wade through the interviews and notes and find the best material to tell the story I wanted to tell. As I wrote, I tried to follow a narrative story arc, with characters, conflict, rising tension, climaxes, and resolutions, in each chapter and overall.

When I think about why I was able to write these books, I think it comes down to obsession. I was obsessed with volcanoes and wanted to learn everything I could about them. But I was also obsessed with storytelling and structure. Considering how to structure a book is the most fun, the most creative, and perhaps the most important part of my writing process.

When I write, I'm like a curator at a museum. I get to decide what to focus on and how to present it. So half the fun is figuring out the answers to these questions: What is the best way to tell this story? What interesting or clever structure will make this amazing material come to life for readers?

TODAY'S ASSIGNMENT

Choose a nonfiction topic, and brainstorm at least three different possible structures for the piece. (I do this before writing my books, though I don't limit myself to only three.)

Ask yourself, Can you tell a story with characters, conflict, and a story arc?

Is there a person with an interesting story who can help you illuminate a topic? If you have a person in mind, what obstacles or conflicts did he or she face? What does he or she want? What stands in the way? What event is the climax, and how is it resolved? I spend a lot of time looking for the elements of a narrative story arc in my nonfiction material.

Can you tell a story that has been missed? Even incredibly well-covered topics such as volcanoes, classical music, the solar system, and the American struggle for civil rights have true stories that have been overlooked for years or decades. Ask yourself, What part of this topic or subject has *not* been covered? You can also ask experts this same question. What do they think has been missed or misrepresented? As you read about your topic, take note of people or events mentioned in passing that sound intriguing—these could became the whole structure for your piece. A brief aside in a newspaper article that mentioned that Wolfgang Mozart had a sister who was also a child prodigy was the genesis for my book *For the Love of Music: The Remarkable Story of Maria Anna Mozart.*

Can you write a mystery story? A story full of suspense? We don't know everything about every topic. Sometimes the most interesting stories surround the unanswered questions. What are the major mysteries about your topic? Has someone devoted his or her life or career to searching for answers to a question? Has the search for truth ever put anyone been in danger? The question *Is it possible that there are more planets in our solar system?* became the organizing principle of my picture book biography *The Planet Hunter: The Story Behind What Happened to Pluto.*

Can you write an adventure story? Everyone, especially kids, loves exciting adventure stories full of cliff-hangers. For the topic that you want to write about, did anyone ever go on a quest or take a perilous journey? Did someone or something have to struggle to defy expectations? Did anyone face danger or even risk death? Thinking of the exploration of Mars as an adventure story helped me decide how to structure *The Mighty Mars Rovers: The Incredible Adventures of Spirit and Opportunity.*

Can you write a love story? Believe it or not, nonfiction can enter into the realm of romance. Somewhere in your topic there may be a story of love, friendship, or loyalty. Will that be the structure that holds your piece together?

Can your piece be funny? Nonfiction doesn't have to be dry or boring. Can you think of a humorous or fun angle? What is the funniest material you can find about your topic? Is there a funny perspective or voice you might want to use?

Does your material suggest a creative structure? Piano sonatas were probably the form of music Maria Anna Mozart played most often, so I decided to structure her story in the form of a piano sonata. The purpose and tone of each part of a sonata helped me choose the material and writing style appropriate for that section of the book. Does the shape of something in your material suggest a shape for your piece of writing?

Encouraging students to consider creative ways to structure a piece of writing can give them a way to really engage with the material and make it their own. If kids come up with creative approaches and structures, they may engage more deeply with the material and, ultimately, write pieces that are more interesting to read. And so will you.

Elizabeth Rusch is the author of more than ten carefully structured books for young readers and more than one hundred magazine articles. Visit her website at www.elizabethrusch.com.

Q+A - THE BEST OF Q-AND-A WEDNESDAY: FINDING SOURCES AND ORGANIZING RESEARCH

Many of our contributing authors proclaim their love of research, but where does a new writer get started? Keeping track of all those notes and sources can be another challenge. Here are some of the best tips we found for finding information and keeping it all organized.

QUESTION: When writing nonfiction books, how do you spend your research time? For example, what sort of sources do you use? Do you conduct interviews? And so on.

ANSWERS:

Research is fun! Yes, I do it all–interviews included. I usually start by taking a look at what's already been written about my subject, and then I spend a considerable amount of time finding my own hook: How will my book be different? What hasn't been said already? I then become a specialist in that subject, which is part of the joy of writing nonfiction for me. Interviews are like gold. They bring personality and expertise into works of nonfiction. What I love even more is getting my hands into whatever I'm writing about so that I can have a firsthand experience with my subject.

~Nancy Castaldo, author of *Sniffer Dogs: How Dogs (and Their Noses) Save the World*

When writing nonfiction, I love talking to people. Oftentimes, they point me in directions I wouldn't ordinarily go. Generally speaking, my research begins on my laptop in my apartment. From there, I go out into the world.

~Phil Bildner, author of *The Soccer Fence*

I love Facebook for research! It's been an amazing way to reconnect with people from my past who are now experts in all sorts of cool fields. For instance, an old college acquaintance is now a professor of evolutionary biology at Harvard, and I email the poor man constantly. Another college friend is an infectious disease specialist. I sent him a ten-page, single-spaced document full of queries for my book in progress. How happy they must be to have reconnected with me! (I'm being facetious, but I do recommend plumbing your past–it's amazing how many people you might know who are experts you can interview!)

~Sarah Albee, author of *Poop Happened: A History of the World from the Bottom Up* and *Bugged: How Insects Changed History*

QUESTION: Does anyone out there have advice on how to go about doing efficient research? I'm particularly interested in how to organize what I find so I can efficiently retrieve the information for current writing projects, but I'd also like to know how to store the information for future reference.

ANSWERS:

Speaking as a nonfiction writer, I like to use www.bibme.org/ whenever I find information in a new source, be it on the Internet or from a book. It helps me keep a well-organized and alphabetized list of my sources. As I type up notes, I always use footnotes in Microsoft Word and just make up a quick acronym for sources I use frequently (such as "BITS, page X" for the book Bugs in the System*).*

For my fiction writing, I use Scrivener to keep notes about character descriptions and settings. I like the ease with which you can whip back and forth from manuscript to outline to character descriptions.

~Sarah Albee, author of *Poop Happened: A History of the World from the Bottom Up* and *Bugged: How Insects Changed History*

It is in the nature of research to be inefficient, especially at the start. But I've tended to organize my research either grouping sources by chapter in which the information appears or by topic.

In my current work in process I'm organizing the research by chapter. Under Chapter 1, I have all the references I looked at for the school system in rural Japan, the cultural information about school and family relationships, the language information about the different names used for grandparents, and titles used for teachers and principals. It also has the information about the Columbia River Bar Pilots Association in Astoria, Oregon, information on tsunamis in general, and about how far out to sea or how far upriver a commercial vessel needs to travel to be safe from a tsunami. I know my editor will be asking me for this information, so having it on hand makes the process go more smoothly.

When I wrote Second Fiddle, *I organized the research according to topic. There was a list of sources for classical music and composition, communism, the Cold War, travel information for Berlin and Paris, and so on.*

I dedicate a section of my bookshelf to books, maps, etc. for each project. I keep a file with links to websites I've used. I keep a list of contacts I've interviewed. I have a file of reference photos for the setting. Those photos have proved useful in offering my editor references for his cover team.

~Rosanne Parry, author of *Written in Stone* and *Heart of a Shepherd*

Q+A - THE BEST OF Q-AND-A WEDNESDAY: TOO MUCH RESEARCH?

Many authors will tell you that research is their very best friend. But research out of control can also be an author's enemy when it comes to getting the writing done. How much is too much?

QUESTION: As authors, how do you keep from getting distracted by what you are uncovering as you research? How do you avoid wasting time on things that come up that are interesting but not about the topic you're researching?

ANSWERS:

I don't think research is ever time wasted, but I know exactly what you mean! Some of my best new ideas come from things I've discovered when I'm doing research. If it is hindering your writing, then I would just set aside time for research (thirty minutes) and then log off the Internet while you write, to avoid temptation.

~Amy Guglielmo, author of Touch the Art series

Ah, I am in the midst of heavy historical research right now. Anybody want to hear about 1830s parlors in southeastern America?

No? No? *What?* It's fascinating!

I'm not sure research is ever wasted unless you find yourself wanting to "research" only when you're feeling reluctant to write. Then it's not research; it's procrastination.

Also, if you treat yourself as a research professional, I think you'll know what's appropriate and helpful to the story–and when to stop. I've tabbed up a half dozen books on my research topics, and now I'm typing notes about how those tabs apply to my story. That keeps me focused on why the heck I'm reading about 1830s America. It's for the story. It's also been helpful, for me, that I drafted the story first, then did the heavy-lifting research. I know what to look for and what I can ignore (as fascinating as 1830s cities in America are, that doesn't apply one bit to my tale, so I skip over that material).

Also, if you find something interesting that doesn't apply to your current tale, save it! I am a big proponent of using Scrivener, and one of the things I love about that application is that you can save entire web pages in a research folder. So toss that web page into a folder, somewhere, somehow, and move along. It'll be ready for the next project.

~Pam Bachorz, author of *Candor* and *Drought*

This is such a huge problem for me. I actually do a presentation called "Confessions of a Research Geek," about finding the balance between research and writing. I tend to want to write novels to answer a question for myself and my readers, so it's very easy for me to find myself in what I call the Research Vortex. What I've learned to do now is when I'm writing a first draft and come across something that needs research, I make a highlighted note [research XYZ] in the manuscript and then do it during a break. I use the Freedom app to cut myself off from the Internet for periods of time while I write.

~Sarah Darer Littman, author of *Want to Go Private?* and *Backlash*

Finding a good and interesting topic is never time wasted, because you never know when it will give you another layer to your story or give you another story idea altogether. If it's not relevant to the story you're writing, tuck it into a folder for future use.

I usually do all my heavy research before I begin writing anything, so being excited about getting going on the story keeps me from spending too much time on research. And then the little things that come up during my writing are usually quick and easy answers that I can look up during little writing breaks.

It also helps that my writing computer doesn't have Internet access, so I can't be tempted to "hop over" to research something real quick while in the middle of my writing.

~Jennifer Brown, author of *Hate List*

CHAPTER 9

Poetry

Nothing strikes fear in the heart of a reluctant writer more than poetry, and that goes for many adult writers as well as kids. All those figures of speech—similes and metaphors, mysterious symbols and personification—can seem overwhelming to readers trying to puzzle out a poem in print, so writing one may feel totally out of reach. But in reality, poetry is a great starting place for new writers, because it offers so much freedom and flexibility. Poems can be simple. They can be short. They can follow strict rules or break them all.

In this chapter, we'll do some poetry warm-ups, play around with a few writing prompts to introduce the genre in a nonthreatening way, and talk a bit about novels in verse, too.

In Lesson 45, poet and author Laurel Snyder shares one of her favorite poetry-writing prompts—a challenge to include surprising elements in a poem—and walks us through a mentor text, showing how this exercise can make an unremarkable poem more vivid and memorable. This is a great lesson to return to when you're working with students on revision strategies for poetry, too.

In Lesson 46, "Clear Thinking About Mixed Feelings," poet Sara Lewis Holmes invites writers to begin a poem with an unexpected idea. Her version, "Potato chips don't go with coffee," sparks a discussion about poetry and the way it challenges us to explore the intersection of thought and feeling.

The power of place can inspire poems, too. In Lesson 47, we begin by reflecting on a beloved place and use the poem "Sometimes on a Mountain in April" as a mentor text. This is another especially accessible poetry lesson to share with students, because the familiarity of a favorite place provides a comfortable starting place for writing. The support of a mentor poem's structure also provides scaffolding to make the assignment feel more manageable. Consider pairing this lesson with those from Chapter 6, on setting and sensory details.

Lesson 48, "Sometimes When I Write," offers a different twist on mentor texts. Instead of using an outside source, writers can use their own thinking processes as a guide. Metacognition is especially helpful for emerging poets of all ages, because it gives voice to the often unspoken processes and emotions of writing.

Finally, our Q-and-A section takes a look at novels in verse—collections of poems that tell a larger story, complete with setting, characters, plot, and theme. Whether you're a beginning poet or an experienced wordsmith hoping to grow, the exercises in this chapter should stretch your thinking in new directions and provide inspiration to share with students as well.

JO'S MORNING WARM-UP

Today I thought we could do a fun exercise my friend Cindy Faughnan (also a teacher) taught me.

First, pick a theme. This can be anything. Some ideas: writing, teaching, summer, parenthood, dogs, friendship, a view you can see right now.

Then, write your phone number down the length of a page, like this:

8

0

2

5

5

5

1

2

1

2

Now start your poem. Each number represents how many words you must have on that line. If you have a zero, that's a wild card, and you can use as many words on that line as you like.

We did this exercise at a summer writing camp, and the students came up with some incredible stuff. This is a really fun one to use in the classroom, because it offers a mix of structure and freedom.

Jo Knowles is the author of *Read Between the Lines, Living with Jackie Chan, See You at Harry's, Pearl, Jumping Off Swings,* and *Lessons from a Dead Girl.* For more of her Morning Warm-Up prompts, visit www.joknowles.com/prompts.htm.

Lesson 45: Poetry Stretch

By Laurel Snyder

One of my very favorite writing prompts is based on something I learned a long time ago, from my poetry teacher in college. Essentially, the goal is to stretch yourself beyond your comfort zone.

For young poets, this is a critical skill, because they often have a very formatted sense of what a poem should be about. They typically think poems are about the natural world. They love birds, the sky, rivers, mountains, lakes, seasons, times of day or night, and so on. They also love to write about feelings: Darkness. Sadness. Blah, blah, blah. Not to mention old places in Europe and broken American landscapes and junk like that.

Of course, poems can be about anything. But "anything" doesn't always feel natural to a young poet, so your students might need fresh inspiration.

TODAY'S ASSIGNMENT

Make a list of things you're unlikely to include in a poem. Categories of things! Mine might be . . .

Electrical appliances

Scientists

Brand names for cereals

Dead presidents

Types of cars

Diseases

Mass murderers

Comic book characters

Something in quotes

Cuss words

Religions not your own

Car parts

State capitals

Words with more than four syllables

Board games

Video games

Things you can find at IKEA

Names of bad hair bands

Scientific names of mushrooms

Sports teams

References to World War I

The goal is to get a certain number of the categories into the poem, using very specific examples of those sports teams and state capitals. Consider setting a target for yourself, such as using five or ten of these things in a poem.

Of course, when you revise, you can always do what you like. Even if you take out the details later, you will have pushed the writing into a new place.

Let's say you set out to write a very typical poem, like this one:

As the
sparrow
falls
through
the gray
sky
above
the river,
I can't help
but think
of you.
Remember?
That night
we walked
the streets
till dawn.
I closed
my eyes
to keep
myself
from
morning.

That poem, or a similar version of it, has been written a jillion times by a jillion college students, pretty much. But what if we add some of the details from my list? We might come up with this:

As the sparrow
falls through the gray Albany

sky above me, I can't help
but think of leprosy.
Why is that?
I guess they both remind me
of you, honey.
Remember that night
we drove your sister's Corolla
too fast, and the
tailpipe fell off?
I do. The Yankees
were on the radio. They had just won.
No surprise there.
But you said you were leaving me.
"Why?" I asked.
"You look too much
like Charles Manson," you told me.
I closed my eyes. And tried
to remember if we were out of
Captain Crunch. Or not.

Admittedly, this is no great poem. But do you see what the items from the list did to the work? They demanded specificity. They demanded that I make a more real relationship for these two characters. They required me to make sense of how incongruous the details themselves were.

If I asked someone else to put Albany, Leprosy, Corolla, Yankees, Tailpipe, Captain Crunch, and Charles Manson in a poem, they'd have to make sense, too, but they'd make a different sense.

This exercise is a lot of fun, and it's especially good to trick yourself out of feeling stuck or bored or blocked in your writing. It doesn't work just with poetry, obviously. You can also try it with a chapter, or you can do this with an outline. Challenge yourself to work details or moments you wouldn't typically write into an outline, and see what that does to the shape of the work. You can keep a running list on your desk or corkboard. Call it "Things I'm Not Likely to Put in a Book."

For picture books, it's a wonderful way to alter the tone of your work. And it can be a neat way to add vocabulary you don't always find in picture books: new words for kids to learn.

Laurel Snyder is the author of many books for kids, including the novels *Bigger than a Bread Box* and *Seven Stories Up*, and the picture books *Baxter, the Pig Who Wanted to Be Kosher*, and *Once a Swan*. Laurel lives in Atlanta. Visit her website at http://laurelsnyder.com.

Lesson 46: Clear Thinking About Mixed Feelings

By Sara Lewis Holmes

One morning, I woke up with the sentence *Potato chips don't go with coffee* in my head.

What a ridiculous, trivial idea.

So, of course, I reached for my pen and notebook and wrote it down. Then I wrote another line. And a few more. Until I "accidentally" wrote this poem:

Potato chips don't go with coffee
My alarm alarmed me with those words.
I told you this, exactly—
and you said:
Led Zeppelin doesn't go with mashed potatoes
and I said:
that's not the same thing!
And you said:
You're alarming me, my sweet, raw potato.

That may not be the most amazing poem I've ever written, but I like it. Why? Because it speaks to how and why we might approach poetry. We write poetry in response to the things that set off alarms inside us, the moments when we are vibrating with wonder, or fear, or heartbreak. Poetry is most definitely *feeling*.

But we also write poetry to examine things more closely—to cry out, That's not the same thing! To logically parse a silly thought until it reveals something we didn't understand when first we were alarmed. Poetry is most definitely *thought*.

Perhaps that's why I love W. H. Auden's definition of poetry as "clear thinking about mixed feelings." So, can writing poetry help you think more clearly about your mixed feelings—whether or not you consider yourself a poet? Can it help you write fiction? Nonfiction? Memoir? I think so.

Let me give you an example. I grew up Catholic, so I know what a credo is. Literally, it means "I believe," and it's a statement of those things you believe in. Many writers earnestly think that this is where they should begin: with what they believe, with what they know for certain, with just the facts, please. I know I did. I wrote many a persuasive essay in school, and I was damn good at it. I could argue the leg off a table, as they say.

But one day, I heard several people toss off the phrase *I don't believe in . . .* , and they weren't talking about theology. They were discussing topics such as wearing synthetic socks, or eating a big breakfast, or buying things online, or giving a child a binky.

When I did a Google search on the phrase, some things that turned up after *I don't believe in . . .* were polls, the death penalty, failure, God, love, atheists, first grade, hell, and walled gardens. (Hmm. That last one intrigues me.)

Then, for my own amusement, I began to riff on the phrase *I don't believe in . . .*

I wound up writing a poem called "Credo," not so much about particular beliefs or nonbeliefs, but about how complicated our personal creeds are. How and why did we draw those lines we won't cross? What are our exceptions? If we had to explain ourselves, could we do it?

Those last three questions—which I never would've stumbled across without writing this poem—could, if well tended, grow into a variety of writing projects: a memoir about my Catholic upbringing, a young adult novel about a particular moral line the main character has crossed (Sara Zarr's stunning *Story of a Girl*, for example), or even a biography of a person whose logical discoveries are at odds with his beloved's faith (I'm thinking of Deborah Heiligman's nonfiction book *Charles and Emma*, about the Darwins).

In Madeleine L'Engle's book *Walking on Water*, she talks about belief this way: "The artist, like the child, is a good believer. The depth and strength of the belief is reflected in the work; if the artist does not believe, then no one else will; no amount of technique will make the responder see truth in something the artist knows to be phony" (1995, 148).

Ferreting out the phony is exactly what poetry is designed to do. Poetry allows you to explore anything you've left unexamined until now, to go to the core of yourself, and to honor both your irrational thoughts and your mixed feelings about what you find.

This is true whether you write poetry for publication—or just because you can. If you'd rather read poetry than write it, that's okay too. (May I suggest two great books? Jeannine Atkins's novel in verse, *Borrowed Names*, in which there is some amazingly beautiful and clear thinking about mothers and daughters, history, and choices; and Joyce Sidman's poetry book for younger ages *This Is Just to Say*, which explores mixed feelings with humor and grace.)

Ready for a poetry-writing stretch?

TODAY'S ASSIGNMENT

Tell me about a time you didn't reject the first silly thought or phrase that came to you, and what happened afterward. Write a poem about it if you wish.

When you have a free evening, find the documentary *Louder Than a Bomb*, which follows four teams of students as they prepare for and compete in a Chicago poetry slam.

Begin a "commonplace book." This is a notebook into which you copy poems you want to keep nearby. You can do this by hand, inking in the lines, or do what I often do: print or make a copy with your computer, and paste it in. Or do both—no rules! Try reading from this commonplace book before you approach your regular writing time, and see if it puts you in the right frame of mind to be both open and clear.

To explore your mixed feelings, write a credo. But do it slant, as Emily Dickinson would advise. Start with "I don't believe in . . ." and see where your intrepid words take you.

PHOTO CREDIT: SONYA SONES

Sara Lewis Holmes is the author of two middle grade novels, *Letters from Rapunzel* and *Operation Yes*. She studied physics at the University of North Carolina at Chapel Hill, government at the College of William and Mary, and writing at home. Visit her website at www.saralewisholmes.com/.

Lesson 47: Sometimes: A Mentor Text

By Kate Messner

Poetry can be intimidating if you've never written it before, and sometimes a mentor text can be just the thing to get a reluctant poet started. When I taught seventh-grade English, George Ella Lyon's "Where I'm From" was a favorite. Students would read the mentor text and then borrow its structure for their own autobiographical poems.

Here's another poem that you can use as a model. I wrote it after an early-spring hike in the Adirondack Mountains (see Figure 9.1).

FIGURE 9.1
Adirondack Mountains

SOMETIMES ON A MOUNTAIN IN APRIL

Sometimes, on a mountain in April,

winter hides in caves.

and clings to warm stone

while spring whispers green promises

in the sun.

Sometimes, on a mountain in April
the rocks are so slippery
you have to slow down
and this is good.
It's when you'll notice
a quiet curtain of moss
that drips with melting snow.

It's when you'll hear the rush
of streams,
swooping up tired old leaves
carrying them off
in dizzy laughter
to somewhere warmer,
open,
free.

Sometimes, on a mountain in April,
you'll slide down slippery rocks
and land in mud.
It's okay.
You'll remember
how black and rich and squishy
and beautiful mountain mud can be.
Don't get up right away.
Dig your fingers in,
and breathe.

Sometimes, on a mountain in April,
if you pause close to the summit,

a butterfly will fly so close
you hear the sound of its wings.
And if you keep listening,
though the butterfly flutters on,
you'll hear quieter things still.
Snow melting on faraway hills,
Insects blinking awake.
Tender ferns unfolding in the sun,

And answers
to questions
You didn't even know you had.

Ready to get writing? Imagine a place that you love. It can be your own kitchen or backyard, a faraway beach, a bustling city market, or a hard-to-reach vista at the end of a hike.

TODAY'S ASSIGNMENT

Start by writing this:

Sometimes, [in your place, on your beach, wherever you are] . . .

Then brainstorm all the things you might *see, hear, smell, feel, taste,* and *wonder* in that place. Feel free to scribble your thoughts in prose or just as a list, or if you want, you can write it as a free-verse poem, using "Sometimes on a Mountain in April" as a mentor text.

Lesson 48: Sometimes When I Write

By Kate Messner

Writing poetry is not only about observing the world by looking out; it's also about looking in, reflecting. After one of our summer Teachers Write workshops, I invited teachers and librarians to share reflections on their own writing, starting with the poetic prompt "Sometimes when I write . . ." Here's a sample response that you might use as a mentor text:

Sometimes when I write, I am frightened I won't be able to come up with anything. I stare at the blank page.

Intimidated

Unsure

Afraid I won't have an idea.

But then I start. Words flow out of my fingertips. My keyboard clicks as I type faster and faster.

Inspired.

Excited.

Curious about what's to come.

And then she comes, that darn annoying voice. My inner editor pops up in my mind.

Criticizing.

Negative.

You can't do this.

At first, I listen. The words slow. But then I shove her out of my mind. I CAN do this. I AM doing this. And all I have to do is keep letting the words come out.

And my fingers start flying once again.

~Katherine Sokolowski

TODAY'S ASSIGNMENT

What does your writing process look like? Spend a little time reflecting, either in prose or poetry, using the first line "Sometimes when I write . . ."

Q+A - THE BEST OF Q-AND-A WEDNESDAY: NOVELS IN VERSE

Often, we think of poetry as a shorter form of writing, but sometimes, poems form the building blocks for a full-length novel. These novels in verse are often lovely and poignant, and they can be popular with bookworms and reluctant readers alike. Here are some thoughts on getting started in writing this unique genre.

QUESTION: What should someone keep in mind if they're writing a novel in verse for the first time? Any tips, suggestions, recommended reading?

ANSWERS:

I think it's important to ask yourself if verse is the best (or even only) way for your story to be told. The spare structure needs to somehow open the story more fully to the reader. I've written several blog posts about writing verse over at my blog, Caroline by line (http://carolinebyline.blogspot.com). Stop by!

~Caroline Starr Rose, author of *May B.*

I remember when I started writing I Heart You, You Haunt Me, *I was so worried about whether I was doing it right, what people would think, etc. Remember that a first draft is a first draft, no matter how you are trying to write it. Get the story down and remember it's for your eyes only. Play and have fun–see what happens.*

Do check out Caroline's blog. I also like this blog post that Kelly Bingham wrote about writing verse novels (click "next entry" when you are finished; the post that follows this is great, too!) at http://thru-the-booth.livejournal.com/134949.html.

~Lisa Schroeder, author of the Charmed Life series

I think Allan Wolf's Newfoundland *is masterful. He has this amazing ability to create images and atmosphere while keeping the action going. I also really love Kelly Bingham's* Shark Girl*. Although it is not entirely in verse, she really effectively uses verse, letters, and diary entries to spotlight different aspects of the story. That's a great book, too!*

~Gigi Amateau, author of *Claiming Georgia Tate* and *Come August, Come Freedom*

CHAPTER 10

I'm Stuck!

"Do you ever get writer's block?" It's one of the most common questions kids ask when I do author visits to schools and libraries, and the answer, of course, is yes. But sometimes we talk about "Writer's Block" as if it were an actual ailment, caused by a specific virus or bacteria, when really, any number of things can stop a writer's productivity.

Sometimes, writer's block stems from a lack of information, and more research is needed. Sometimes, it's a matter of returning to an earlier stage in the writing process to do some brainstorming or free writing. Sometimes, it reflects a crisis of confidence. In all cases, the key to being a writer is writing anyway.

In this chapter, we'll take a look at some of the struggles writers of all ages face, whether they're beginners or award-winning authors, and explore some strategies for getting past writer's block and getting back to work.

In Lesson 49, "Wordle: What Am I Writing About?" guest author Barb Rosenstock shares a fun, visual strategy that makes use of technology to get writers thinking about their work in new ways. The online tool Wordle will take any block of text, from a short poem to a full novel, and create a visual representation of the work, with the most frequently used words and ideas highlighted by size. This is a great tool for writers who are struggling to identify the most important themes in a work in progress, and it's a favorite of student writers, especially when the graphic Wordle image is published alongside the final written product.

Sometimes, feeling stuck is a matter of not knowing what happens next in a story. In Lesson 50, "The Stop and Block," guest author Shutta Crum offers a concrete strategy for pushing forward when a writer is unsure what path his or her character might take next. This is not only a great trick for getting "unstuck" but a useful revision strategy as well.

Guest author Joanne Levy offers another take on the "What happens next?" dilemma in Lesson 51, "The Worst That Could Happen." She challenges authors to move a story forward by imagining the worst possible situation a character could be in, plopping him or her squarely in the center of that problem, and then watching how he or she reacts. Try this lesson with students when they feel stuck writing a rough draft or when they're revising a piece to try to make the plot more interesting.

Sometimes, the answer to writer's block lies not within the draft of writing itself but in some time away from the work. In Lesson 52, "Getting Unstuck," guest author D. Dina Friedman offers some ideas for stepping away from a piece to get the creative juices flowing again.

The middle is the most dangerous place for a writer. Many writers simply give up and put the project aside when they discover that the shiny allure of the original idea has worn off, the characters have been around a while, and the ideas aren't coming as quickly. But whether you're working on a research project or a short story, pushing through that "muddy middle" is essential to finishing a draft that can then be revised into a piece that shines. In Lesson 53, "Moving Forward," guest author Karen Day offers some tips for staying focused and some strategies for plowing ahead.

Finally, Lesson 54 is called "The Ultimate Cures for Writer's Block." (This is the one you were waiting for, right?) Part of winning the war against writer's block is identifying the enemy, and here, we'll take a look at different reasons why writers get stuck and how each one offers a particular path to writing again.

JO'S MORNING WARM-UP

In one sentence, tell me why your story is important to you.

If you haven't started a story yet, tell me why writing is important to you. In fact, you should answer this question either way.

Once you have your sentence(s), post them in your workspace or on your computer or in your writer's notebook—somewhere you will see your statement(s) every time you sit down to write. Let these words guide you every day as you work toward reaching your goal.

Jo Knowles is the author of *Read Between the Lines, Living with Jackie Chan, See You at Harry's, Pearl, Jumping Off Swings,* and *Lessons from a Dead Girl*. For more of her Morning Warm-Up prompts, visit www.joknowles.com/prompts.htm.

Lesson 49: Wordle: What Am I Writing About?

By Barb Rosenstock

I was in the middle of drafting a picture book and had just pasted and deleted essentially the same two sentences six times. I thought I'd created interesting characters, a cool setting, and the basic plot outline, but where was my theme? (I can still hear my fourth-grade teacher, Mr. Fornek.) Was this a story about friendship? Or courage? Or plain cleanliness? Here's a way that might help you figure out what you're writing about when you're stuck.

TODAY'S ASSIGNMENT

Go to www.wordle.net. It's free, and you don't have to fill in personal information or sign up. If you haven't used Wordle before, it's a tool that generates a graphic word cloud from text you insert. The Wordle is based on frequency of use in your text. Click "create," and paste in a good chunk of text from your work in progress (at least two pages.) Hit the "Go" button.

Surprise! You'll see a pretty Wordle graphic generated from your very own writing. Now look at which words are bigger and which are smaller, and notice which are missing altogether. Are you writing about what you think you're writing about? You may find that the word *friend* shows up the largest, that nothing describing your setting shows up at all, or that a minor character's name comes out larger than a major one—all useful information for finding a theme and revising.

If you're feeling super-motivated today, write a letter to or from your main character using the seven largest words in your Wordle.

My theme is invention. What's yours?

You can do this exercise with any writing: your journal, your work in progress . . . even one or two of your quick-writes combined.

Barb Rosenstock loves true stories best. She lives outside of Chicago with one husband, two sons, and two big poodles. Barb loves to visit schools and encourage student writers. Her picture books are *The Camping Trip That Changed America, Fearless, The Littlest Mountain, Thomas Jefferson Builds a Library, The Noisy Paintbox, The Streak,* and *Ben Franklin's Big Splash.* Visit her website at www.barbrosenstock.com.

Lesson 50: The Stop and Block

By Shutta Crum

I'm a believer of getting your characters into jams and firmly eliminating "easy out" alternative choices along the way, so that your character(s) *must* choose the path you want him/her/them upon. Too often, we writers—once we know where we want the story to end up—take off headlong in that direction, getting our characters into all kinds of problematic situations and forgetting the important second half of this technique. That second half involves blocking off the other paths—paths that reasonable people (characters) might take, given the circumstances of the moment. By eliminating these options, you will make it more likely that your reader will suspend any disbelief and travel along happily for the ride . . . er, read.

TODAY'S ASSIGNMENT

Choose two characters you are working with, and a setting. Or simply pick three words from the dictionary, at least one pertaining to a character and one to a setting. (Randomly, I chose *cinema*, *furrier*, and *incurable*.)

Do a five-minute "automatic" write. No rewriting or editing is allowed. Write whatever comes to mind. Don't wrap up the scene.

Stop at a point where the primary character is about to do something important. (My incurably insane/romantic furrier has just walked into a cinema with a mink stole he made for the woman of his dreams. He notices she is attending the movie with another man. I stop.)

List four or five actions your character could take at this point, whether these seem reasonable or crazy.

Choose one of the more unlikely actions for your character.

Choose another action that is reasonable.

Now start writing again with the intention of making your character's crazy choice seem logical at the moment and, more important, making the reasonable choice seem illogical. (My choices: The furrier could realize she is not for him and walk away, walk away and decide to get his revenge later, accost the man/woman, drape his stole around the woman and try to pull her into his arms, or pull a pistol from beneath the mink stole. Hmm . . . The reasonable choices are to walk away—even if he's insane. He could get revenge another day, if he wants. So I need to block those choices. Perhaps the asylum attendants are looking for him and they are just outside the entrance? Okay. So I write a line or two indicating why he can't walk away . . . Now I can write on. "Slowly he . . .")

Repeat this process, stopping, listing, and blocking periodically as you work on your manuscripts to make sure you've tied up all the loose ends. Then your readers won't complain, "But wait! Why didn't he just . . . ?"

Shutta Crum writes picture books, novels, and poetry. She is also a storyteller, a public speaker, and a librarian. Her articles about writing have appeared in many professional journals. Her book *Thunder-Boomer!* (Clarion 2009) was chosen by the American Library Association and *Smithsonian* magazine as a Notable Book. *Mine!* (Albert A. Knopf 2011) was listed in the *New York Times* as one of the best board books of the year. Visit her website at http://shutta.com/.

Lesson 51: The Worst That Could Happen

By Joanne Levy

Here's a question to ask yourself when you're stuck in the middle of a draft: What's the worst that could happen now?

Back when I was dipping my toe into the writing pond, I took some courses at the local college to prepare. I'd always loved to write, but I knew nothing about craft or how to make an okay story into a *great* story; I needed help. I learned a lot in those writing courses, especially because the workshop approach enabled me to get feedback from my teachers and peers. A couple of pointed lessons really stuck with me.

One is that you have to *kick your main character*. Repeatedly.

"Noooooo," you say. "I love my character! I want only the best for her. Sunshine and light and all things rose smelling." But if you're writing a story, no matter if it's short or an epic tome, you need to kick your character a few times. You need her to grow, thrive, and shine, and it's only by overcoming high-stakes obstacles that she will triumph. (Some characters don't grow, thrive, and shine, but fail and come apart when faced with hardship. But I'm going to assume that many of us are writing for kids where there is a positive or hopeful, if not happy, ending. In any case, characters still must deal with hardship, so this exercise is still valid; you'll just have a less than positive outcome.)

So, think of the worst that can happen to your character. And then make it happen.

My very favorite example of this is the movie *Castaway*, with Tom Hanks. Watch it (you can call it research!) and see how many times poor Tom gets kicked. Hard. And the way he gets kicked is brilliant, too, in that good news/bad news way:

> *Good news: You survived a plane crash. Bad news: You're stuck on a deserted island, by yourself.*
>
> *Good news: You found new shoes that you desperately need. Bad news: You have to take them off the corpse of your buddy.*
>
> *Good news: You get the shoes off. Bad news: They're too small. (Some kicks are big, some are small, but they all still count.)*

And it goes on and on. But through hardships we grow and show our true colors—these are life's pivotal moments. As writers, we use these moments to make our characters human and sympathetic. We love them *more* for what they have overcome, right? It's hard to love a character who has everything handed to her (and it makes for a boring story). Where's the grit? The strength, the stuff that makes you root for her?

TODAY'S ASSIGNMENT

Take your character, thinking about her most debilitating fears or faults, and make the worst possible thing happen.

Is your character a terribly shy introvert? Force her to do a speech in front of a thousand people.

Is your character deathly afraid of snakes? Put him in a pit full of them (remember Indiana Jones?).

You get what I mean. Kick your character and see what happens. I bet you'll learn a little something more about her that you didn't know before; maybe she fails miserably, or maybe she can succeed and come out the other side stronger.

And when that happens, you know what to do: kick her again.

Joanne Levy is the author of *Small Medium at Large*. A survivor of the corporate world, Joanne lives in Ontario, Canada, with her husband and a lot of pets, one of which vomited during the writing of this bio. Visit her website at www.joannelevy.com.

Lesson 52: Getting Unstuck

By D. Dina Friedman

When I'm stuck, I generally do one of two things.

I thumb through a book of poetry, writing down lines that appeal to me. It's important not to think, *Oh, I could write a poem about this*, or *This would be a good thing to say about my character*. I try to simply pick lines that intrigue me, and then free-write whatever images they might bring up. Here are two lines that have worked well for me, but if they don't work for you, feel free to pick your own.

The day is a woman who loves you. (Richard Hugo)

When the wind ended . . . (William Stafford)

Try free writing about either of these lines and see what you come up with.

A variation of the first-line exercise is to pick a line that can repeat itself and use that as a jumping-off point. When you get stuck, come back to the original words, generating a list. Some good lines to start with:

I remember . . .

If only . . .

I believe in . . .

A second thing I tend to do when I'm stuck is look out the window, especially if I'm not at home. "Writing landscapes" helps me home in on the key details, which are often the small, unnoticed things: dust particles in the sunlight, a crumpled leaf, the bird dropping that is staining a cracked brick step. I try to start by simply describing what I'm seeing, but I let that writing take me to different places. The initial attempt at literal description helps me refine my visual skills and also challenges me to use evocative, sensory language that goes beyond the physical details and helps to convey metaphor and mood.

TODAY'S ASSIGNMENT

Look out the window, and write what you see, down to the last, tiny detail. Let that writing take you wherever it leads.

If your window does not jazz you, you can do the same thing by thumbing through a book of landscape photographs. Give it a try and see what details come forth in the images.

D. Dina Friedman's novels are *Escaping into the Night* and *Playing Dad's Song*. She grew up in New York City. Visit her website at http://ddinafriedman.com/.

Lesson 53: Moving Forward

By Karen Day

You finally started that novel you always wanted to write. You brainstormed, made an outline, found a main character and plot. You set aside time to work. You made progress; several chapters are written (and it was easier than you anticipated)! You feel good about it. Inspired! You can't wait to wake up and work.

Then one day, perhaps quite suddenly, something changes. Your main character seems flat. The tension has fizzled. The plot has disappeared. You don't know where to go, what to do. You forget what your piece is about. You get discouraged. You weed the garden and clean your closet. You decide not to write for a couple of days. You think you have to start over. You wonder if you're a writer after all.

Does any part of this sound familiar?

If so, do not despair. You're experiencing something that every writer, both published and unpublished, experiences. Expect to be lost multiple times while writing your first or second or even third draft. It's part of the job. Don't let it scare you.

To help, I thought I'd give you a couple of suggestions to keep you going when times get tough. I often resort to one or two (or all of them) when I'm working on early drafts. Hang in there. Take a deep breath. And don't give up!

When writing a first draft, you must write every day. This will keep your story fresh in your conscious and unconscious mind. Don't worry if all you have is fifteen minutes. Sometimes you can get a lot done in short amounts of time. The important thing is consistency and forward momentum.

Don't circle back and rewrite early chapters until you have a draft finished. When writing, I always keep paper next to my computer where I list the changes I'll make in the next draft. If you continually make changes, you'll never finish a draft. Besides, how can you rewrite the opening chapter when you don't know exactly how your book will end?

Which leads me to this point . . . A first draft is an ugly mess that I wouldn't even show my dog. It's filled with holes, melodrama, and threads that appear and disappear with no resolution. It's terrible. That's terrific! Because revision is where the real writing occurs. But you can't revise until you have something to work with.

I lose track of my main theme/themes when I write, so I always write the main ones (two or three) on a piece of paper that I tape to my computer. For example, while writing *A Million Miles from Boston*, I had this on my computer: "Lucy believes (mostly unconsciously) that accepting change in her life means rejecting her dead mother." When I got stuck, or wondered why I was writing a particular scene, I'd look at that paper and ask myself, How does this scene fit with my theme/themes? Or does it?

Sometimes I'll be sixty pages into a manuscript and lose my way. Then, writing an entire chapter seems daunting. So I tell myself that I'll write just a scene: A conversation with the antagonist. A resolution. Something my main character discovers. I might write ten pages or more of these short "scenes." From these new paths, I can usually get myself going again. Don't worry if this part of your manuscript doesn't look like the other parts. Remember, it's a draft!

At different places in a draft, I'll stop and assess. Has my plot shifted? Do my characters want different things than I thought they did? Is the antagonist no longer the antagonist? This is okay, of course, but you might try to write up a new synopsis. It will help you stay focused.

Maybe you've tried these suggestions, and others, before and nothing has worked. You're still stuck. How do you know when to abandon something? Several times I've been fifty or sixty pages into a book, then put it aside. But I never totally abandon anything. I might pull out characters or plots and use them elsewhere. Sometimes when you're stuck, it's because your story isn't quite right. The setting is off. Or maybe the wrong character is telling the story.

Be open to new possibilities, but don't worry about what you leave behind. No writing is ever wasted.

TODAY'S ASSIGNMENT

If you feel stuck, and none of these other suggestions work, try writing a couple of chapters from your antagonist's point of view, or from a minor character's point of view. Is this awkward? Easier? Should the entire story be told from this different point of view? Or does the exercise help you see your original narrator more clearly?

Karen Day is a teacher and author of the middle grade novels *Tall Tales*, *No Cream Puffs*, and *A Million Miles from Boston*. Her novels have appeared on numerous lists, including Bank Street College Educators Best Books of the Year. She has taught writing workshops at the Cape Cod Writing Center conference, the Chautauqua Institute, and Grub Street. Visit her website at www.klday.com.

Q+A - THE BEST OF Q-AND-A WEDNESDAY: DEALING WITH DOUBT

It happens to every author somewhere along the journey. You're writing along happily, but in the middle of the draft, doubt creeps in and sits down beside you. Maybe you imagine that negative voice in your head, whispering things like, *This isn't good enough,* or *Who do you think you are, trying to write a book/article/dissertation?* Writers who succeed in finishing projects have a variety of strategies for dealing with that doubt and deciding which voices to heed along the way.

QUESTION: How do you deal with doubt in your writing? When you get help with your work, whose feedback do you trust?

ANSWERS:

Doubt is a great thing for any artist (and writers are artists). It means you're jumping into something new. If I decide to write a horror story, I'm comfortable, and I know I can do it because I've written many of them. I'll create good work, but I won't grow as an artist. (Let me emphasize that there's nothing wrong with this. We need to jog between sprints.)

But if I decide I want to write a realistic novel about a boy who wants to work as a clown in a dunk tank, my first thought will be, I can't pull this off. I've never written this sort of book.*Then I have to sit down and push through the fear–assuming my need to write that book is great enough. Every time I've pushed past the doubt, I've been glad I did–even if, in the end, I didn't finish the book for some other reason. I spent four years avoiding a book I wanted to write because I didn't think I could make it interesting. (It's fiction about math.) I finally sat down and wrote a test chapter. Then I wrote the book. Acknowledge that doubt is a real force, and take it not as a stop sign, but as a challenge.*

~ David Lubar, author of *Hidden Talents* and the Weenies short-story collections

Doubt stinks, but it's part of the process, at least for me. In fact, I was just doubting my ability to write a coherent sentence this morning. I think when you doubt your words, your ideas, or yourself, you're really wondering, Do I have anything meaningful to say? *which isn't a bad question to ask. The answer is always yes, we all have important stories to tell (whether we write them down or not). But depending on what you're working on, the doubt might be coming from not having found your path to or through the story. That's the process part, the "don't give up, try again, keep searching" part. If you weren't a thinker, you wouldn't be a teacher or a writer. Thinkers question, wonder, and doubt. It's often the place where the good writing comes from. If you can, get the book* Art and Fear *by David Bayles and Ted Orland. Read it and keep it close; it helps.*

As for the feedback question, I'm odd in that I don't belong to a formal writing critique group. I spent a lot of years in advertising having my writing critiqued by committee, so I tend to not do group critiques. Sometimes I'll try something out on my husband, and I do have three or four "writer friends" to whom I send drafts if I feel something's missing (and they send drafts to me). Their opinions can be tough to hear, but I trust them completely. Maybe you can hook up with some other teacher-writers?

~Barb Rosenstock, author of *The Camping Trip That Changed America* and *The Noisy Paintbox*

Doubt is a tricky little monster, and he always seems to be around! Every now and then, I remind myself, This is not life or death. This is just a book. *It helps to remind myself that if this particular story stinks, it is not the end of my world. It is not even the end of my writing. There are always more ideas where this one came from. Also, trust your instinct. You're a reader, so you know what good writing looks like. If the writing looks good to you, you're probably right!*

As for whom I trust for feedback on my work . . . I can't trust my husband. There, I said it. He's just so stinkin' nice, he would never tell me if something wasn't good. Cheerleaders are great, but they're not very helpful in improving your work. So I usually don't let my husband or my parents read my work until it's through revisions. I do have a critique partner, and also a select couple of author friends I'll ask for help every now and again. And then my agent will give honest editorial feedback as well. Find yourself a like-minded writing buddy who will tell you when something needs to be changed but will do it in a way that won't crush your soul.

~Jennifer Brown, author of *Hate List*

Doubt is entirely normal—so pat yourself on the back for experiencing one of the genuine and shared pains of writers everywhere. If you didn't have doubt, chances are you'd be too confident in your writing and wouldn't do the hard work necessary to make your writing the best it can be. So, if possible, embrace your doubt . . . but don't let it paralyze you.

Gather a group of trusted readers and get the feedback you need to take your writing to the next level. Figure out what's working and celebrate that. Then figure out what's not working and why. By embracing the process step-by-step, the large, looming cloud of an unfinished project becomes a series of manageable components.

Share your work with a small, experienced group of writers and readers. Here are a few questions that might help you determine whom you can trust:

Does their feedback nag at you, prompting you to ask many more questions until you understand what the real issue is?

Do they start with what's working and what's not and then turn to rules and resources to clarify their thinking? Or do they start with the rules and try to fix things that may not be bro-

ken? Hint: I worry about the latter.

Are their comments generally consistent with those of other trusted readers?

And finally, do they know how to ask the big *questions, about tension, pacing, character, and so on?*

~Jean Reidy, author of *Too Purpley!* and *Light Up the Night*

I deal with doubt by knowing that it is part of life when it comes to writing. There will always be those voices that creep into your head while you're writing, saying, That's no good *or* Boy, honey . . . you might as well hang this up now and take up basket weaving. *For me, the trick is recognizing when those old songs are playing and saying,* Ah . . . I know you. Okay, pipe down for a while so I can get to work.

Whose feedback to trust is often a matter of trial and error, and you may need to critique with someone for a while before you figure out if his or her feedback works for you. You don't want someone who just pats you on the head and says how great your book is; you want someone who can push you to make it better. And on the flip side, you also can't really trust the feedback of someone who consistently makes you feed bad about yourself. I hate to even bring this up, but I know friends who have been in critique groups where ego and frustration might combine to make a writer's feedback more of the tear-it-down variety than the let's-build-it-up kind. You want good, tough, constructive feedback, not negative energy.

Probably the best way to tell if feedback is good is to try what's being suggested. Does your critique partner think you should delete a character? Rewrite the beginning? Change a plot thread? Try it with an open mind (in a separate document, so your old version is still there). Does it make sense to you? Do you feel good about how it turned out? If this happens pretty consistently, you've probably found someone whose feedback you can trust.

And one last thing—this is why it's a good idea to have multiple readers for your work. If one of my critique partners suggests something and I think, Hmm . . . I don't like that, *I'll often wait to see what the others say. If no one else mentions the issue, it may be a personal preference, but if another one points out the same thing, I know that I have work to do, and an issue to resolve, even if I choose to resolve it in a way that's different from what the first partner suggested.*

~Kate Messner, author of *All the Answers, How to Read a Story*, and the Ranger in Time series

Q+A - THE BEST OF Q-AND-A WEDNESDAY: WRITER'S BLOCK

If you've ever picked up a pencil or started a new document on your computer, you've probably experienced writer's block. It's that awful feeling of being stuck and incapable of moving forward. How can a writer get past this stage? Our guest authors have some thoughts.

QUESTION: I'd love to hear about your experiences with writer's block, and some of the ways you were able to move past this frustrating phenomenon.

ANSWERS:

I think most writers experience times when the idea well feels a bit dry. The thing is, though, you have to push through it. One of the ways I do that is to get up and move. I will sometimes go for a walk, but I will more often blare some music and dance around my office. I'll often choose a song my character would relate to.

Another thing I do is draw a picture of the scene I am trying to write. Now, let me tell you, I draw like my hands are wrapped in duct tape. Horrible. So, we're just talking stick figures here. But often, that simple image creates a Technicolor one in my head. (If I got the same picture in my head, I'd be in deep trouble.)

I also find that sometimes going back to other parts of the manuscript and reading aloud will kick-start ideas. But mostly, I just write stuff I know isn't working, and I keep going! In that five or six pages of drivel, I'll often find one sentence that's good enough to become its own chapter. Ironically, some of my favorite chapters have come from those times.

~Lynda Mullaly Hunt, author of *One for the Murphys* and *Fish in a Tree*

I think about this one a lot. Sometimes when I have trouble writing, it's just a general resistance to the task of writing. My inner critic can be really discouraging, and it's easy to come up with a million little tasks that delay writing time until there is no time left.

To get past writing resistance, I start with a little ritual like lighting a candle or writing the date, something that's really easy to do. Or I write with a timer: so many minutes on, then a break, then another session. I like to write in chunks of twenty-five minutes. It's long enough to get stuff done, but short enough that it doesn't feel overwhelming.

Sometimes though, the reason I'm struggling with writing has nothing to do with resistance. I'm showing up, I want to write, and I can't think of anything to say. Nine times out of ten when this happens, it means I've taken a wrong turn in my story somewhere. If I back up, reread, think about whether my characters are really acting true to themselves or I made them do something just to move the plot along, I'll find the place I've veered off course, and I'll be able to continue.

–Jenny Meyerhoff, author of *Third Grade Baby* and *The Barftastic Life of Louie Burger*

I think getting writer's block is similar to getting muscle cramps and soreness when you first start exercising. As you get into better shape, you get fewer and fewer aches and pains. Writing really is like exercising a muscle, except that you train your brain to do it. If I get stuck, I step away for a while (run, walk the dog, read a book). Usually an idea comes to me, but if it doesn't, I write something crappy. Better to write than not to write, and better (I think) to have something than nothing, because you can always fix it at the revision phase!

–Sarah Albee, author of *Poop Happened: A History of the World from the Bottom Up* and *Bugged: How Insects Changed History*

Q+A - THE BEST OF Q-AND-A WEDNESDAY: THINKING ABOUT TITLES

Whatever you're writing—a novel, a short story, or a poem—the title makes a promise to readers about what is to come. Sometimes authors title a piece before they write another word, but often, titles can be challenging and might not be final until long into the revision process. Our guest authors offer some thoughts on brainstorming title ideas.

QUESTION: This may seem like a simple question, but it is one that is a pain in my side. Titles: How do you come up with something that is original, yet draws a reader in?

ANSWERS:

Titles either come really easily to me or they are impossible. I do think when you're starting out, a great title can make an agent or editor sit up and take notice. However, it's not the end of the world if you can't come up with something spectacular. Titles often end up getting changed by the publisher anyway.

Look for a phrase in the manuscript that is especially meaningful or gets at the heart of the story. Because of Winn-Dixie *by Kate DiCamillo is about a preacher's kid, but there is a dog she names Winn Dixie, and it plays a key role in getting Opal connected with all the special people in that novel.*

When I brainstormed names of the cupcake shop and came up with the idea of It's Raining Cupcakes, *I knew it would be the perfect title for the book. I've learned over the years that the* *more you try to make it special and unique and memorable, the better it will work. I actually love the titles of Jennifer Smith's latest YA novels, because they are fun, unique, and memorable (*The Improbability of Love at First Sight *and* This Is What Happy Looks Like*). Go for words that make someone sit up and take notice.*

~Lisa Schroeder, author of the Charmed Life series

I title books and chapters the same way–and they usually come when I am not searching for them. One for the Murphys *was originally titled* Clip, *until I came to the place in the books where I typed the phrase* one for the Murphys. *As soon as I did, I froze, knowing that it was the new title.*

I try to do a few things when choosing a title. It should raise questions in the mind of a reader–that is, spark interest. If it's a phrase that can be taken in more than one way, that's good–or a play on words. It's nice when a title can serve as an overarching description or metaphor for a book. One for the Murphys *is a layered meaning in the book. It's also a red herring. Lastly, a lyrical title is nice; Jennifer Smith nails that!*

~Lynda Mullaly Hunt, author of *One for the Murphys* and *Fish in a Tree*

CHAPTER 11

Revising and Critiquing

When I visit classrooms or Skype with student writers to discuss my writing process, I always ask the kids, "How many of you have traded papers with a friend to get ideas on how to make your writing better?" Most hands go up, including mine. Students are first surprised, and then delighted, to hear that published authors engage in this same kind of collaboration. Writing can be a quiet, solitary process, especially in the early stages of brainstorming, planning, and drafting, but later on, it is almost always helpful to have input from a reader who is also a fellow writer.

Some writers, especially students, dread the thought of revision. "But I'm *done*!" is a common refrain in classrooms. Yet if we think about revision from the very beginning, if we approach it as an essential, productive, and satisfying part of the writing process, something magical happens. Writers begin to see that the very best writing happens in the rewriting stage.

It's no secret that revision is my favorite part of the writing process. I love it so much that I wrote a whole book about it. Teachers who write to me say that *Real Revision: Authors' Strategies to Share with Student Writers* (Stenhouse 2011) has become a favorite, dog-eared reference for their classrooms. In this chapter, we'll just scratch the surface of the revision process, exploring some strategies for revising in the kind of shared writing community that might be found in a classroom or in a study group for educators.

Revision through collaboration and feedback was a central piece of our summer Teachers Write workshops. In Lesson 55, "The Story of Friday Feedback," author Gae Polisner invites writers into the online critique group she created so that writers of all levels could find that sense of community and get constructive criticism on their work. Gae shares specific strategies such as the positive-first approach and flash edits, as well as general guidelines for creating a similar setting for feedback in your writing group or classroom.

In the real world of publishing, authors receive feedback not just from other writers but from their editors as well. In Lesson 56, "Editor in Training," Chronicle Books editor Melissa Manlove shares the actual editorial letter guidelines that she uses to train interns in how to give feedback to authors. Melissa's suggestions provide a "behind the curtain" look at publishing, and you can share these strategies with student writers, too.

Before authors send their work to editors, they've already revised their writing multiple times, often with help from peers. In Lesson 57, "Writers' Critique Groups," guest author Natalie Dias Lorenzi shares how her group formed and evolved. She offers thoughts for writers who may want to be part of a similar community.

In Lesson 58, "More on Critique Groups," we explore the different kinds of writing groups that can form—in person and online—and how they work.

Lesson 55: The Story of Friday Feedback

By Gae Polisner

In October 2009, after nearly ten years of writing, submitting, and endless rejection, I got my first traditional book deal on so-*not*-my-first manuscript, *The Pull of Gravity*. Before that, most of my writing took place in solitude, without much feedback, save for a few willing family members and friends. As such, I wrote and read hundreds of thousands of my words subjectively, without much objective feedback about whether or not they were compelling, authentic, or good.

In December 2010, having secured both an agent and finally, a book deal (as well as much positive "traditional" publishing feedback on several of my manuscripts), I felt like I had something to offer other aspiring writers. I started a feature on my blog called Friday Feedback.

WHY FRIDAY FEEDBACK?

First and foremost, I thought, the idea behind Friday Feedback would be "Brave is as brave does." I decided to include a brief (three- to five-paragraph) excerpt of my own writing from a work in progress (WIP) in the main body of the post, and invite my readers/commenters to give me specific feedback, based on these questions: Does it "hook" you or compel you to read more? What works about it? What, if anything, doesn't?

Then, if they wanted, I'd invite them to put up a brief excerpt from their own WIP in the comments, and I—and any of my readers who cared to chime in—would offer the same feedback.

If I was encouraging others to post, I knew it was important to first find the pearls in each person's writing. And, yes, there are always pearls. In this way, I hoped I might help them find conviction in their own unique writing style and voice.

Once those pearls were discussed, I would offer some simple "constructive" criticism that I hoped would encourage contributors to keep going and motivate them to improve.

In that first December 2010 post, I wrote the following:

> *Why am I so excited about this? Writers often write in a vacuum. As such, you'll often hear us commenting that we have no idea if something we've written is great, or if it's crap. I mean, you'd think we'd know, but sometimes, honestly, we just don't. Sometimes, the chasm of doubt we stare down is that gaping and wide.*

Something amazing happened when I put up that first post. People showed up to my blog and participated in the comments. My hunch was correct: there were aspiring writers who wanted and needed their words to be read, and they craved honest and encouraging feedback. More and more people started contributing each week. Our collaboration seemed to help newer writers not only learn some basic writing tips and improve their revision process but also get better as a whole.

A second important thing happened as well: the English teachers who frequented my blog because of the *Of Mice and Men* tie-in to my first book, *The Pull of Gravity,* commented that they were becoming more aware as critics of their students' work. As they waited for feedback on their excerpts, they understood for the first time how anxious their students might feel after turning work in to their teachers. They also understood the importance and value of offering positive comments first.

Writing is vastly personal and intimate. If we can provide some honest praise first, then I believe we are more open to accepting any constructive criticism that might follow. In contrast, receiving criticism first often causes us to shut down, blocking further progress. If this is true for professional, adult writers, imagine how true it must be for tweens and teens still finding their self-esteem. It's certainly why I enforce one of the few rules of *Friday Feedback*: tell me what works about the piece *first, before* you tell me what doesn't.

One of my favorite parts of *Friday Feedback* is finding excerpts that lend themselves to what I call a Super-Speed Flash Edit (see Figure 11.1). With the permission of contributors, I take an excerpt and perform a five-minute revision, *never* for substantive content or voice, but solely for those common pitfalls that might bog down the writing or take away from its flow. Common pitfalls are extra, repetitive, or unnecessary words and unnatural dialogue tags that "pop the reader out of the story." The most important thing about these edits is that they are not intended to change the writer's own voice or style

Suddenly the two men captured Lira's attention as they straightened, Jarvin reaching for the sword at his side. Barth was slower in his response but within a few heartbeats both had their weapons out and looking through the trees off to their left. Moving to her knees, Lira didn't rise because there was a strangers suddenly rushed into their camp. Almost immediately, Jarvin took a step forward and met two of them with a clash of steel. Lira jerked at the sound and watched in horror as two others engaged Barth. Two men stood back in the shadows, their weapons drawn but not attacking.

A feeling that she was needed enveloped Lira, but she couldn't think of what to do. She stifled a scream when Jarvin's sword found it's mark and one of the men he was fighting stumbled backwards only to be replace by the other two. Barth seemed to be holding his own, but the intensity of fighting by his opponents was lacking compared to Jarvin's.

Suddenly one of the men lunged forward and his sword

The two men captured Lira's attention as they straightened, Jarvin reaching for the sword at his side. Barth was slower but, within a few heartbeats, both had their weapons out, aimed through the trees. Lira dropped to her knees as the strangers rushed the camp. Jarvin took a step forward and met two of them with a clash of steel. Lira jerked at the sound, and watched in horror as two others engaged Barth. Two men stood back in the shadows, their weapons drawn, but held.

Enveloped in fear, Lira felt helpless. She stifled a scream when Jarvin's sword found its mark. The man stumbled backwards, only to be replaced by two others. Barth seemed to hold his own, but his opponents' intensity lacked compared to the men attacking Jarvin.

Suddenly one of the men lunged forward and his sword found its mark, slashing Jarvin across the leg. Jarvin stumbled, but managed to stay upright. The paralysis that had stopped Lira fell away, and she breathed deeply, gathering power from the air around her. She let a chain of lightning streak towards the man who had dared strike her friend. He fell with a stunned gasp,

FIGURE 11.1
Before and after

in any way, but rather to let that voice or style stand out and shine. Through this process I help the writers "see" what I mean rather than struggle with some unclear explanation of how, what, where, or why they should make a certain edit. *Res ipsa loquitur. The thing speaks for itself.*

TODAY'S ASSIGNMENT

Are you ready to get feedback on your work? If you're writing with a group or partner, choose a short piece to share, with the goal of providing feedback to one another. Remember, share something that works first, and then provide constructive feedback! If you're writing on your own, ask a trusted friend to read your work and answer these questions:

Does it "hook" you or compel you to read more?

What works?

What, if anything, doesn't?

Gae Polisner is the award-winning author of *The Pull of Gravity* and *The Summer of Letting Go*. She is a family law mediator by trade but a writer by calling. She lives on Long Island with her husband, two sons, and a small dog she swore she'd never own. When she's not writing, she can be found in a pool or, in warmer weather, in her wet suit in the open waters of Long Island. Visit her website at http://gaepolisner.com.

Lesson 56: Editor in Training

By Kate Messner with Melissa Manlove of Chronicle Books

Some of the best advice I've ever heard for offering critiques to developing writers came from my Chronicle Books editor, Melissa Manlove. She frequently trains new interns in the Chronicle editorial department, but her guidelines are useful for anyone who critiques writing for a friend, colleague, or student. Melissa says:

> *Critique is useless when it is vague. I want to pinch people in critique groups when I hear, "This is so cute." Critique is also useless if it is entirely positive or entirely negative. Neither kind of response will help writers move forward and improve their*

work. Critique should always begin with specific, positive feedback. This is important for several reasons. Here's what I wrote for our interns about giving editorial feedback:

HOW TO WRITE AN EDITORIAL LETTER

1. Start with the best. Identify the strengths of the book, the things to which the book's audience will most connect. All of them. Be specific.
   a. Because these qualities will be your pole star as you guide the book through the publishing process. Books change as they are developed. Having iterated to yourself at the beginning what the point and value of the book is will help you ask yourself whether each change along the way serves the true nature of the book.
   b. Because when you iterate those things to the author, you gain the author's trust. Authors are absolutely right to distrust anyone who does not see why the book is valuable yet wants to suggest changes. And authors are facing the difficult and sometimes painful process of revision. The admiration and excitement of a knowledgeable stranger—you—gives them fortitude and faith in the face of that process.
   c. Because if you don't iterate those things to the author, the author might change them during revision. Never assume the author sees the brilliance of their book, no matter how obvious it is to you. This is no criticism of authors—it is their job to see the trees. It is our job to see the forest.
2. Remind the author to argue with you. Remind the author that you want to hear her point of view, and to help her make this the book she wants it to be. This also builds trust, because it communicates that the author is in this process with a respectful partner—not with a general who will command or with a surgeon who will cut. Neither war nor medicine is a creative process. And this openness to disagreement builds trust because it communicates that you are not in this to make it the book you want it to be, but simply the best book it can be. There is no ownership in editing.
3. Ask questions. Editorial confidence opens pathways and facilitates decision-making, but editorial inflexibility is the enemy of creativity.
4. Point out problems, and explain specifically why you believe they are problems. But suggest solutions as questions. A suggested solution can help the author to understand better how you perceive the problem. But remember that the best solutions usually come from the author. Specifically communicate that if the author has different ideas for how to approach each issue, they are very welcome.

5. Think of each book as a thing of its own, with a soul and identity apart from any of the people involved in it. What does the book want to be?
6. Be grateful. We are each of us absurdly lucky to be working in this field.

TODAY'S ASSIGNMENT

What suggestions might you add to Melissa's critique guidelines if you were sharing them with a critique group? How might you adapt her guidelines to share with students?

Melissa Manlove is an editor at Chronicle Books in San Francisco. Her acquisitions tend to be for all ages in nonfiction and from infancy to age eight for fiction. When acquiring books, she looks for fresh takes on familiar topics as well as the new and unusual. An effective approach and strong, graceful writing are important to her. Melissa also has sixteen years of children's bookselling experience.

Lesson 57: Writers' Critique Groups

By Natalie Dias Lorenzi

It can be scary sometimes when we put our thoughts and feelings on paper. But *sharing* those thoughts and feelings? With strangers? Now, that's terrifying.

There are some authors who don't share their writing at all; no one sees their manuscripts except for their editors. And this works well for them. But me? I can't imagine bringing a story into this world without feedback from my critique group.

Back in 2005, I was a few chapters into a manuscript, which would later (seven years later, to be exact) become my first middle grade novel, *Flying the Dragon*. I had joined SCBWI (the Society of Children's Book Writers and Illustrators) and perused the message boards trying to learn all I could about the craft of writing. One day I came across a message from another writer, Kip Wilson Rechea, who was looking to fill an open spot in her critique group. I emailed her with my first chapter, as requested, and waited. Would she hate my writing? Would she chortle at my beginner's prose? Luckily for me, she did neither; instead, she invited me to join her critique group.

During that first year, members came and went, but eventually our group settled into four writers: Kip, Julie Phillipps, Joan Paquette, and myself. A few years ago, we came up with a name for our group: the Lit Wits. Every Wednesday for the past seven years (give or take a Wednesday or two), one of us submits pages to the group via email. The others leave comments within the text itself as well as a paragraph of their overall thoughts and impressions.

Other writers have asked me how we've kept our group together for so many years. If any of you are interested in forming a critique group, this is what I'd recommend:

1. *Get to know other writers.* **The SCBWI discussion boards provide a great forum for kid lit writers: www.scbwi.org/boards/. Although I hadn't met Kip before responding to her call for a new critique group member, I did get to know Joan through an online writing course before she joined the group. You just might find a critique partner or two in your local community of writers.**
2. *Join writers who are at a similar stage of writing.* **When my group started, we were at the beginning of our writing careers. Over the last seven years, our writing has been published in magazines and anthologies, and we have picture books, middle grade, and young adult books now out on the shelves. This isn't to say that a beginning writer and a published writer can't be in the same group. In larger, in-person critique groups, there's often a greater mix of writers who swap manuscripts or snippets of stories. But in general, I recommend finding a group with at least one other member who is at a similar point along the writing path as you are.**
3. *Decide on a method that works for your group.* **We decided to submit no more than ten pages per week. We had one critique partner who is such a prolific writer that she left the group because she needed full-manuscript swaps, not ten-page submissions every month or so. She spends a lot of time outlining first, but when she's ready to write, she cranks out at least a thousand words a day and finishes a first draft in a few months. Neither method is wrong; just decide which one works for you, and find others who feel the same way.**
4. *Give constructive feedback.* **This seems obvious, but it isn't always easy to do. We tell one another what works, what's funny, what touched us, and what didn't make any sense whatsoever. If you were to look at our critiques, you'd see comments like these:**

stumbled over this line–maybe reword?

This doesn't sound like her–would she really say that?

Lovely!

We had one critique group member years ago who said only positive things about our writing. She is a lovely person, but she wasn't helping anyone grow as a writer. She ended up amicably parting ways with the group, which was a good thing in the end. (If I want to hear all good things about my writing, I'll share it with my mom.) If you want to grow as a writer, you'll need to hear what works and what doesn't work from your readers.

Being a part of the Lit Wits has definitely informed my teaching. When it's time for one of my students to share his or her writing, I understand—*really* understand—how intimidating that experience can be. As a writer, I also understand what kinds of comments help me become a better writer. We need to hear what we do well, and we need to hear, in a constructive and supportive way, what isn't working.

If you flip to the acknowledgments page in any children's novel, you'll almost always read the names of those who have helped shape a manuscript into a story. Joan (who writes as A. J. Paquette) sums it up perfectly in the end pages of her middle grade novel *Rules for Ghosting*: "[To] the many others who have had a hand in critiquing, guiding, shaping, idea-brainstorming, and otherwise helping make this story what it is, I couldn't have done it without you" (2013, 260). Joan goes on to name the members of the Lit Wits and other critique partners.

TODAY'S ASSIGNMENT

Brainstorm a list of people who might be critique partners for you, or reflect a bit on how you might go about getting feedback on your work. Best of luck to you all in finding whatever type of feedback works best for you. I look forward to one day peeking at the acknowledgments section of your books!

Natalie Dias Lorenzi is the author of *Flying the Dragon*, a middle grade novel published in

2012 by Charlesbridge. She is an elementary school teacher-librarian near Washington, D.C., and a contributing writer for Scholastic's *Instructor* magazine. Her essays appear in two anthologies: *Teacher Miracles: Inspirational True Stories from the Classroom* and *Break These Rules: 35 YA Authors on Speaking Up, Standing Out, and Being Yourself.* Visit her website at www.nataliediaslorenzi.com.

Lesson 58: More on Critique Groups

By Kate Messner

There's no doubt that having another set of eyes on your writing can help you improve your work. That's where critique groups come into play, where the writing process becomes not solitary but social.

A critique group is a small group of people (usually two to six) who write and agree to read one another's work from time to time and provide feedback with the purpose of helping one another improve. Critique groups can happen in person—if you live close to some other writers, you might agree to meet once a month at the local coffee shop—or online, in which case you'd exchange pages of writing via email or set up a system with folders in Yahoo Groups or something similar.

The groups can be made up of people who are at about the same level (beginners, folks revising first novels, and so on), people who write the same genre (young adult, middle grades, picture books, nonfiction) or people who write different kinds of work but have an appreciation for what the others write, too.

Sometimes, critique groups operate on a schedule (each week, writers take turns sending maybe five pages for critique by the others), and sometimes they're more informal (people share work when it's finished or when they need feedback, and others critique as they can; this is more common with experienced writers, I think, who tend to have deadlines and less predictable schedules).

Sometimes, it takes a while to find the right critique group. People sometimes post new critique groups or openings in established ones on the SCBWI discussion boards. Sometimes, you might express interest in a group, and someone else has filled the spot already or seems to be a better fit for that particular group. *Do not take this personally or read anything into it at all.* It happened to me numerous times when I was looking for a critique group, and if it happens to you, it doesn't mean that you're not a good writer or nice person or anything else. It only means that your "just-right" critique group is still out there. And sometimes, people join a critique group and then realize it's not a good fit, so they drift away. All of this is part of the process, and it's okay.

My current group consists of writers who focus on different genres, but we appreciate one another's work. We run into each other at conferences and retreats sometimes, but our group operates mostly online (via Yahoo Groups), and we don't have a set schedule. I also have a few other writer friends with whom I swap manuscripts sometimes.

TODAY'S ASSIGNMENT

Do you think you might like to be in a critique group? Take a little time to brainstorm the kinds of feedback you'd like to receive on your writing and what kind of group might be the best fit for you.

Q+A - THE BEST OF Q-AND-A WEDNESDAY: MAKING REVISION FUN AND TACKLING CLICHÉS

Sometimes, when kids finish a piece of writing, they see the first draft as the only draft and are reluctant to revise. (The truth is, some adult writers feel the same way!) Breaking revision into smaller tasks can help make the process more manageable and even fun. A writer might make a separate revision pass, for example, looking only for dreaded clichés, to replace them with more original, vivid phrases.

QUESTION: I was wondering if any of you have any unusual activities that you use when you are revising your work. Revising can be very difficult for sixth graders (actually, for all ages), so I was hoping for some activities to make revising (I can't believe that I am going to use this word) fun.

ANSWERS:

One of the first things I do after finishing a draft is to read back through and make a synopsis on paper—I know, this is kind of backward! It's fun for me because I assign every plot thread (or, in some cases, different characters) a different color and get to break out my colored pens (cheap thrills, what can I say). After I finish, I can see with a quick scan whether I'm dropping threads, if there's too much orange in one section, if I haven't mentioned that purple thread for five chapters, if I started a green thread but dropped it completely halfway through, etc. I've found it really helps with balance.

~Megan Miranda, author of *Fracture* and *Hysteria*

Ask the kids to bring in a drawing they did in first or second grade. After they've shared their art and had a good laugh, point out that at the time they did the drawing, they probably thought it was perfect. Tell them that they will feel the same way about what they are writing if they look back at it in four or five years.

Give them an adverbial phrase, such as talked loudly, *and then give them a minute or two to see how many action verbs they can write down to replace the phrase. See who came up with the most. Write a list on the board.*

Have them write an essay or story at the beginning of the year. Collect their work and put it aside for a month. Hand it back and ask them to find one or two things they'd like to change or improve. (With luck, they'll be able to view the work in a different way than if they'd tried to revise the day after writing it.)

Tell them that working writers love revision.

~David Lubar, author of *Hidden Talents* and the Weenies short story collections

I often make a storyboard for my book after I've finished a draft. I learned this method from Carolyn Coman, so I can't take credit. Basically, for each chapter of the book, I make one box. In the box, I draw the strongest image I see when I visualize the chapter. Above the box, I write the strongest emotion. Below the box, I write a three- or four-word phrase that encapsulates what happens in the chapter. I fit all of the chapters/boxes on one big sheet of paper. This lets me "see" the book—the flow of it, the emotional arc of it. Now, your students probably aren't writing full-length books. But if they are writing short stories, they could break them into scenes and make a storyboard from the scenes. It's a great way for them to narrow down the most important elements of their stories.

~Jo Knowles, author of *Living with Jackie Chan* and *See You at Harry's*

QUESTION: I'm curious how you all feel about clichés. Do you weed them out as you draft or let them take root? Do you make them a priority for revision or leave other readers—editors, maybe—to sound any cliché alarms? Any winning methods for helping students get the cliché concept?

ANSWERS:

Busted! I'm guilty as charged. Wait . . . That's a cliché. Those little buggers just seem to sneak into a story when you're not looking. Did I just do it again? Maybe a lesson in finding clichés *starts with* What's a cliché? *I absolutely try to revise and remove any clichés from my writing before it goes to other readers. Maybe a class story using only clichés would be a funny way to show students that they can always find a more original way of saying something.*

~Amy Guglielmo, author of the Touch the Art series

I wonder whether it might be difficult for students to recognize clichés because they've had less exposure to them than adults. To take a parallel example, because I've been reading science fiction all my life, I know enough not to write a story where the last two survivors on Earth happen to be named Adam and Eve. That's a cliché in the genre. But a kid might not know that, and might write such a story. There's nothing wrong with that.

I guess a lot of the answer depends on the age of the students. For elementary school, I'd say just let the words fly. For middle school, suggest they try to say things in new ways.

~David Lubar, author of *Hidden Talents* and the Weenies short story collections

I'll let the clichés fly if I'm drafting and nothing else comes to mind as I go. I try not to slow down initial drafts with internal editing. However, I take a hard eye when I revise, and try to remove them all. Thank goodness for my critique partner, though, who will catch anything I miss.

~Pam Bachorz, author of *Candor* and *Drought*

As a former humor writer, I have spent countless hours rewriting clichés for humorous purposes. You might try an exercise where, as a class, you do that. Write out (or brainstorm, as a class) a list of clichés, and then come up with a different way of saying them that's exaggerated for humor (the only example coming to mind at the moment is kind of crass, but would definitely get giggles: shaking like a leaf *turns into* shaking like a dog pooping peach seeds*). The humor will keep them interested, and ideally the exercise will get the point across that there are lots of ways to say things.*

Also, I think kids may not be as aware of clichés as adults are. Having a master list that they can refer to while writing might be helpful.

~Jennifer Brown, author of *Hate List*

Cliché busting is definitely a revision thing for me. The Inner Critic Lady will certainly look down her nose through her monocle and note them as I write the first draft, but if I can't think of something better immediately, I won't stop to fret. Just repeat the mantra, That is what revision is for.

~Sarah Darer Littman, author of *Want to Go Private?* and *Backlash*

Q+A - THE BEST OF Q-AND-A WEDNESDAY: CRITIQUE GROUPS

Critique groups are a little like small neighborhoods: each one is different, with its own social rules and personality. You'll notice this in the comments our guest authors shared in response to a question about critique group stories during our summer Teachers Write workshops.

QUESTION: What, in your opinion, is the best, most effective number of people to work in a critique group? I'm in the air about whether to assign critique groups to my students or encourage them to form organically. Does anyone have an opinion on this or has anyone seen it work spectacularly in either form?

How often do you schedule time with your critique group, and is that time enough?

When you hand your work to your critique group, do you go in with a preset idea of what you want from their feedback, a set of consistent rules/guidelines for critique, or is it more free-flowing?

And finally, when you think about how the most useful pieces of criticism are couched, are there any common things about them that stand out in your mind (tone, content, length, and so on)?

ANSWERS:

With my middle school and high school students, I called the groups writing teams—mainly because the word critique *made them think they were going to trash everyone's work. Sometimes we'd use a response sheet for them to fill in and give to the teammate. Or they would pass the paper around and write directly on that, using one of the responses below.*

Our rules:

1. Be nice or be neutral.
2. Use a quiet voice when talking to your partners, so other teams can work, too.
3. Choose how you'd like to respond from the following list of responses:
    - You've used some strong images such as ____________________.
    - I like the part about ____________________.
    - You've followed the format by ____________________.
    - Great work so far! What if ____________________?
    - The part that really caught my attention was ____________________.

4. If a team member is reading aloud to the group, use your listening skills:

   Give the reader 100 percent of your attention.

   Look at the reader.

   Keep hands empty and still.

   (Talking, writing, clicking pens looking away, etc., are distracting to all.)

~Erin Dealey, author of *Deck the Walls*

I'm not a teacher, but I definitely think a format would be helpful. That way everyone's on the same page about the kind of critique they're going to get, and it keeps the discussion from derailing (something I've seen in adult groups a lot, too).

In my own critique experiences, I've found that a group with more than six or seven people is unwieldy. More than that and there's no time to get everyone's feedback on everything. We meet once a month because that fits best into everyone's life and gives us time to read things in advance. I definitely think once a week is too much if you're doing critiques in advance of the meeting, because then all you do is critique and there's not much time for writing.

~Miriam Forster, author of *City of a Thousand Dolls*

CHAPTER 12

Time to Reflect

This book was a long time in the making. I'd spent months pulling together lessons and writing prompts, questions and answers, and quotes before I approached my editor to see if the project might work. When she gave the green light, I spent more weeks organizing ideas and files and images, setting the table so that I could sit down and write.

On one of the coldest days of the year, I began the introduction. *Lake Champlain froze this week . . .*

On that day, the ice was calling to me in its guttural, otherworldly voice to leave the keyboard, to go outside and skate. But that would have been a lousy way to start a book aimed at moving writers to write. So I stayed at my desk until my words were written for the day. (Later, there was time for skating. The temperature had crept above zero by then, and the fresh air was all the more satisfying with that first file saved on my hard drive.)

Many weeks and twelve chapters later, I find myself at the same desk, fighting all the same battles. Upstairs, the kitchen needs tidying, and just outside my window, the snow is finally starting to melt a bit. It is the first day of spring, and the eight-year-old in me is bouncing in her chair even as I type. It looks like more fun outside. And I'm hungry, too. Isn't it lunchtime yet?

As always, there are so many reasons not to write.

But there are also reasons to write—bigger, better reasons that go far beyond the editor, patiently waiting for my manuscript. Writing this book has reminded me of the joy in the journey, the importance of celebrating process, for ourselves and for the writers we teach. When we write alongside them, we are more than teachers; we are mentors and travelers on the same rocky path of the writing process.

In these final pages, I hope you'll take some time to reflect. During our summer Teachers Write camp, educators asked our guest authors to share their best advice with young writers. You'll find their responses here, and no doubt, after all these days of writing, you'll have new ideas of your own to share as well.

You'll also find one last writing prompt: "A Letter Through Time." I hope it will inspire you to reflect on this journey of words you've taken with me and all the guest authors who threw open the doors to their own writing worlds. I hope it will help you celebrate how brave you've been in putting words on paper, how much you've accomplished and learned and grown. And I hope you'll share that celebration with a writer friend or two and keep encouraging one another, even as you encourage your students.

Most of all, I hope you'll keep writing.

JO'S MORNING WARM-UP

Begin with these words: "I want my words to . . ."

See where it takes you.

Lesson 59: A Letter Through Time

By Kate Messner

To me, one of the greatest gifts of writing is the way it nudges us to look more closely not only at the world but also at ourselves. When we turn the lens inward, we have the chance to reflect, an opportunity to think about where we've come from, where we are, where we are going. When we model this kind of reflective writing, we become mentors for our students as well. We invite them to slow down, turn off their various electronics, and listen to the quiet of self.

Presumably, you're tackling this prompt toward the end of your writing apprenticeship. Maybe you've been spinning words together with colleagues for a semester or simply making a commitment to write on your own, a little each day. You're a different writer from the one you were when you first picked up this book. And right now, you're being granted some special time-travel abilities for this final prompt.

Write a letter to yourself as you were the day before you started these weeks of writing. That letter will be sent back through time and delivered to you the day before you pick up this book. What advice will you give yourself? What can you tell yourself about what the experience will be like and how it might change your writing or teaching?

When we first launched the Teachers Write virtual summer writing camp in 2012, I completed this prompt at the end of August, along with hundreds of teachers who had joined us for that first summer of writing together. Here's what I wrote:

Dear Kate,

Today, you are going to notice some of your Twitter teacher-friends talking about their goals to write this summer, and it will occur to you that it might be fun to set up a virtual writing camp. Go ahead and do it, even though it's not going to go the way you're imagining. You're probably picturing a dozen people, right? Maybe twenty? Multiply that by fifty and you'll be a little closer. It'll freak you out at first when you see all those people signing up, but don't worry–they are amazing people who will be happy to be here and patient with your summer schedule. Besides, tons of generous and talented authors are going to show up to pitch in. This probably doesn't surprise you, does it? The children's and YA writer community is amazing like that.

What will surprise you is just how much you are moved when you sit down to read the comments every day. These teachers and librarians will be so smart, so brave. They will try new things. Some will be afraid at first, but they will be so good to one another, so supportive, that new voices will emerge every week. And these voices will be full of passion and beauty, humor and joy, and poignancy. They will be amazing, and they will make you cry sometimes, in the best possible way.

So go on . . . Write that introductory blog post, even though you're biting off way more than you know. It will be worth every second, and when August comes, you will not be ready to let go. Not even close.

~Kate

And here are some of the reflections that our teachers wrote at the end of that summer.

Dear Margaret,

You have committed yourself to writing this summer, but what does that really mean? You've signed up for the Teachers Write camp. What were you thinking? Did you realize that in the beginning you will be shy and lurk around, reading others' writing without sharing? Don't worry. You'll get over it and jump in, and when you do, the responses you receive will keep you going in for more. You will meet and learn from many wonderful new authors. You will feel a part of the writing world, no longer alone, hanging out with friends. Don't hesitate to go over for Friday Feedback. You have a new friend and cheerleader waiting there for you. And when you come to the end of the camp, you will feel tired and invigorated all at the same time. Also, you will be asked to do your own real writing workshop with teachers, and because you've been here all summer, you will have new and fun things to share with your colleagues about teaching writing, not to mention the great ideas you will have for your own classroom. So, go ahead: go to writing camp!

~Margaret Simon

Dear Andy,

This is the first summer in eleven years that you will not be teaching summer school. It is appalling that the district cut such an unbelievable summer program for elementary kids. Don't get too depressed, though, because a golden opportunity to move your own writing ahead and learn from some of the best young adult and middle grade authors in the world is right in front of you. Teachers Write will lead you to your best summer of writing and learning that you have ever had.

Make sure that you set realistic writing goals for yourself, because you want this opportunity to feel successful in the end. Also, be sure to take good notes and pay close attention to all the published authors who will share their writing secrets with you. By the end of the program, you will have dozens of writing activities that will complement the writing lessons that you already use in your classroom. And most important, read what the other campers are writing and offer critical but encouraging feedback like you would to your own sixth-grade students. It is also important to make some friends who are going through the same things that you are as a teacher, a reader, and a writer.

By the end of the summer, you will be a more confident writer, a well-prepared writing teacher, will have read many novels from the authors who shared lessons, and will have met some very cool people.

~Andy Starowicz

Dear Amy,

You have seen an invitation to participate in this special opportunity called Teachers Write, a virtual summer writing camp. You don't know it yet, but you are going to learn so much about writing and the things writers do to inspire their work, finding inspiration in the everyday, progressing through research, revising, setting goals and sharing your work in an online community of others who will be supportive to a newbie writer just like you.

Here is some advice as you prepare for camp:

1. Prepare to write every day–but make your program work for you. You know that having your seven-year-old and nineteen-month-old children will put demands on your time that may pull you away from your writing work, but get back to it when you can.

2. Share what you are doing with others.

3. Learn all you can from this community of experts–authors, teachers, and librarians.

4. Don't be afraid to take risks, like the motto on your blog–"a ship in port is safe but that's not what ships are for."

5. At some point work up enough self-confidence to join a critique group (if you don't get to this point, it's okay–just keep working at it).

6. Remember, the best writers are also avid readers (make time to read, too). You may have to give up watching TV. Take something off your plate to get all of this done. The effort you put into it will pay off someday.

7. Write every day.

8. Write every day.

9. Write every day.

10. And write every day–even if it's just for fifteen minutes.

You may not always be able to do all ten things on your list, but try. Oh, and if you do nothing else, write every day! So, you're off and away to camp real soon. Enjoy the learning, you "virtual Teachers Write camper," you!

On your mark, get set, write!

~Amy Rudd

Dear Erika,

Just do it! You know that you want to sign up for camp, especially writing camp. You always wonder how other teachers feel like teaching writing is easier than teaching reading, so this is your chance to get a little bit better. Summers always feel a combination of endless and limited, but you definitely need a few goals to keep you hopping this summer. So, even if you do not participate much, remember that you are living what you teach–being a lifelong learner means stretching and growing. You love reading, so learning from all the amazing authors will give you connections to even more awesome authors.

Best,

~ Erika Victor

Dear Susan,

Get the excuses out of the way first–not enough time, not enough talent, not enough to say. You know deep down in the pit of your stomach that you really, really want to do this: writing whenever and however you can, no pressure at all, with talented people who only want you to succeed. How can you possibly say no to that? (And think about those seventh graders in the fall–how will you let them know you only want them to succeed, too? You surely will learn some tips about that process here.)

Perhaps it will turn out that you really do have something to say and people are actually interested in your words and in sharing their words, which in turn will give you more to think about. Perhaps you will learn how a single encouraging word (even if it's said to someone else) can make all the difference. Perhaps you will grow your writing muscles so that you come from a place of strength when the kids come into your classroom. Perhaps it will be good to feel what they feel–the excitement, the anxiety, the fear, the dread, and the pride. Perhaps you can learn from other teachers and writers how to make it more about the excitement and the pride.

Who knows? It might even feel like coming home. Do it.

~Susan McGilvray

TODAY'S ASSIGNMENT

It's your turn now. Put today's date on the paper, and then write your message to be sent to yourself, back through time. What will you take away from these weeks of writing? What will you hold close for yourself? And what will you take back to your students?

Q+A - THE BEST OF Q-AND-A WEDNESDAY: ADVICE FOR YOUNG WRITERS

When we write for our students, we create models for them to follow in their projects. When we write with our students, we truly become their mentors, part of our classroom community of writers. Author mentors can be a part of that community, too. Here, they share some advice for the next generation.

QUESTION: What advice (in one or two sentences) would you offer a young sixth-grade writer?

ANSWERS:

You can't polish a blank page.

~David Lubar, author of *Hidden Talents* and the Weenies short story collections

Read a lot of books. Sample different genres and flavors.

Write about something you care about, or something that you'd like to read.

Write. Write. Write. Read some more.

~Amy Guglielmo, author of the Touch the Art series

Live a rich life. Try lots of different things, and hang out with lots of different people–because that will always *inform your writing.*

~Pam Bachorz, author of *Candor* and *Drought*

Be constantly inquisitive and aware of the world around you. Ask questions. Listen to the news. Read. Talk to people who are older than you, younger than you, from different backgrounds and cultures. You never know where and when the idea will hit you–but you have to be open to it when it does.

~Sarah Darer Littman, author of *Want to Go Private?* and *Backlash*

You need to write something–anything at all–before you can write something great. That's tough sometimes because the ideas we have are great and lofty, while first drafts can be ugly. But that's what revision is for.

~Kate Messner, author of *All the Answers, How to Read a Story,* and *Ranger in Time* series

There is never a wrong answer to What if . . . ?

~Jennifer Brown, author of *Hate List*

Step 1: Put butt in chair.

Showing up is the most important part, in writing, in life.

~Barb Rosenstock, author of *The Camping Trip That Changed America* and *The Noisy Paint Box*

Recommended Resources

Atkins, Jeannine. 2010. *Borrowed Names: Poems About Laura Ingalls Wilder, Madam C. J. Walker, Marie Curie, and Their Daughters.* New York: Henry Holt.

Bayles, David, and Ted Orland. 2001. *Art and Fear: Observations on the Perils (and Rewards) of Artmaking.* Santa Barbara, CA: Capra.

Cameron, Julia. 1997. *The Artist's Way.* New York: Putnam.

Edgerton, Les. 2007. *Hooked: Write Fiction That Grabs Readers at Page One and Never Lets Them Go.* Cincinnati, OH: Writer's Digest Books.

Ellis, Sherry, and Laurie Lamson, ed. 2011. *Now Write! Mysteries.* New York: Tarcher.

Gerke, Jeff. 2010. *Plot Versus Character: A Balanced Approach to Writing Great Fiction.* Cincinnati, OH: Writer's Digest Books.

Gilbert, Elizabeth. 2009. "Your Elusive Creative Genius." TED Talk. www.ted.com/talks/elizabeth_gilbert_on_genius.

Grafton, Sue, ed. 2002. *Writing Mysteries.* Cincinnati, OH: Writer's Digest Books.

Heiligman, Deborah. 2011. *Charles and Emma: The Darwins' Leap of Faith.* New York: Henry Holt.

King, Stephen. 2000. *On Writing–A Memoir of the Craft.* New York: Scribner.

Lamott, Anne. 1995. *Bird by Bird: Some Instructions on Writing and Life.* New York: Anchor Books.

Leguin, Ursula. 1998. *Steering the Craft: Exercises and Discussions on Story Writing for the Lone Navigator or the Mutinous Crew.* Portland, OR: Eighth Mountain Press.

L'Engle, Madeleine. 2001. *Walking on Water: Reflections on Faith and Art.* Wheaton, IL: H. Shaw.

Lewis Holmes, Sara. 2007. "Credo." http://saralewisholmes.blogspot.com/2007/10/poetry-friday-credo.html.

Louder Than a Bomb. 2011. Documentary. Siskel/Jacobs Productions.

Sidman, Joyce. 2007. *This Is Just to Say: Poems of Apology and Forgiveness.* Boston: HMH Books for Young Readers.

Snyder, Blake. 2005. *Save the Cat: The Last Book on Screenwriting You'll Ever Need.* Studio City, CA: Michael Wiese Productions.

Weiner, Jonathan. 1994. *The Beak of the Finch: A Story of Evolution in Our Time.* New York: Knopf.

Whitford Paul, Ann. 2009. *Writing Picture Books: A Hands-On Guide from Story Creation to Publication.* Cincinnati, OH: Writer's Digest Books.

Zarr, Sara. 2008. *Story of a Girl.* New York: Little, Brown Books for Young Readers.

Index